AMERICAN JUSTICE

IS AMERICA A JUST SOCIETY?

OPPOSING VIEWPOINTS SERIES: Volume Nine

Gary E. McCuen

GREENHAVEN PRESS, INC.
ANOKA, MINNESOTA 55303

© 1975 by Greenhaven Press, Inc.

ISBN 0-912616-15-6 Paper Edition
ISBN 0-912616-34-2 Cloth Edition

TABLE OF CONTENTS

TABLE OF EXERCISES

A major emphasis of this book is on critical thinking skills. Discussion exercises are included after readings to stimulate class discussion and individual critical thinking.

INTRODUCTION

With the public knowledge of the Watergate scandals and their aftermath, concern has grown over the question of justice in America. Serious issues have been raised concerning not only our legal institutions but also our social, economic, and political institutions. This volume presents a debate concerning the broad issues of American justice and how people are treated by our nation at home and abroad. It examines American behavior, values and institutions in relation to our concept of criminal, economic and social justice. Basic questions are raised about the definition of justice, how it has been applied in American society and how it should be implemented in the future.

The **Opposing Viewpoints** format and **Discussion Activities** are vital aspects of this book. These features help teachers and students explore the kind of mind-set, skills, and attitudes that are necessary for intelligent analysis of magazines, newspapers, books,

1

and all kinds of printed matter. This format also should help raise some of the following questions:

1. How many people are aware that three of the most popular weekly news magazines, **Time**, **Newsweek**, and **U.S. News & World Report** have a political slant and are not objective accounts of the news?

2. How many readers know there is no such thing as an objective author, book, newspaper or magazine?

3. How many people think that because a magazine or article is unsigned it is a statement of facts rather than opinions?

4. How can one determine the political slant of newspapers and magazines?

5. How does the editorial page of a newspaper differ from the other pages?

6. How many readers question an author's **frame of reference** (his training, political persuasion, and life experiences) when they read a book?

No doubt many people finish their formal education unable to cope with most of these basic questions. At best they will have little chance to understand the social forces and issues surrounding them. At worst one might say they have not received an education in any meaningful sense of that term. And some may fall victim to demagogues that preach solutions to problems by scapegoating minorities with conspiratorial and paranoid explanations of complex social issues.

The editor does not wish to imply that anything is inherently wrong with authors and publications that have a political slant or bias. All authors have a frame of reference because they are human, and readers should understand this reality. The **discussion exercises** after readings deal with separating **fact from opinion, bias from reason, primary from secondary sources, how to empathize,** and **how to recognize stereotyping, scapegoating, and ethnocentrism.** These discussion exercises along with the **Opposing Viewpoints** format hopefully will introduce students to the kind of questions they must ask and the skills they must learn to rationally analyze and interpret what they read.

1 CHAPTER

CRIMINAL JUSTICE

Readings

CRIMINAL JUSTICE: A PUNITIVE SYSTEM THAT NEEDS REFORMING

Ken Jackson

Ken Jackson has served as president of the Fortune Society, an organization of ex-convicts in New York City that promotes reform of prisons and our criminal justice system. The Fortune Society publishes **Fortune News**, a publication that deals with the problems of prisons. Ken Jackson was one of 12 ex-convicts brought together for a conference sponsored by the Academy for Contemporary Problems. The 12 ex-offenders presented the following position paper to the Academy.

Think about the following questions while you read:

1. What myths does Jackson say are promoted by the criminal justice system?
2. What does he say about punishment?
3. What changes does the author recommend for the criminal justice system?
4. How does the cartoon in this reading support the author's ideas?

Ken Jackson, "Ex-Con Coalition Offers Blueprint," **Fortune News**, June, 1974, p. 2.

We cannot continue to address issues regarding the criminal justice system in isolation from the larger issues confronting our society. The criminal justice system in general, and the correctional system in particular, is reflective of the inequalities prevailing throughout our society. The system is **un**just: the majority of incarcerated "offenders" are poor, disadvantaged, or minority group representatives, and their incarceration creates institutional ghettos which are reflective of the **racist, sexist** and economic values prevailing in our society. The only common denominator of these constituencies is that they have no voice or recognition in the so-called democratic process.

As ex-prisoners who have gone through the maze of the criminal justice system in America, we would like to express our concerns and comments towards influencing the course of change which must take place in the correctional system if it is to ever become a system of justice instead of **in**justice.

We feel that we have a contribution to make which must be considered by anyone who seriously desires such a change. For we represent the captive population that has traditionally been manipulated, used, and often abused to gratify the needs and political ambitions of a small number of persons who in the name of social protection have acted in an extremely antisocial manner.

We shall state some of our concerns which must be explored in an attempt to end the wasteful and destructive drain of lives, tax dollars and energy which is now being expended on one of America's most unsocial institutions.

Myths

The criminal justice system, under the pretense of dispensing justice, has perpetrated and promoted numerous myths. These myths both delude a society into believing it has an effective correctional system and prevent necessary reform. Some of these myths are:

• Convicts are violent, illiterate agitators; they are sick and deranged people.

5

• Corrections has a developed body of effective techniques for treatment and care of incarcerated individuals.

• Corrections must protect the rights of individual prisoners; therefore, only corrections officials should have access to correctional decision-making.

• Corrections has adequate facilities and programs to provide human care.

• Long sentences in correctional institutions deter prisoners from returning to crime.

These myths are perpetuated under the guise of administering justice, when in reality corrections is justifying its own existence.

These myths, perpetrated by the criminal justice system, have created a false sense of security as well as a dependence on an "out of sight, out of mind" correctional philosophy. Only the process of violence, confrontation and investigation have provided realistic information to the public about prisons. We are advocating the need for change. We demand criminal justice that provides society with truthful statements about its knowledge and capabilities of working with convicted persons. We must inform the public of inadequate and unjust systems and dispel the myths that prevent change.

Because we are advocating a new direction in criminal justice, we must also become advocates for social change in our larger society. We must challenge the myths of corrections, the judiciary, law enforcement and the American way of mediocrity in our society. If society is to protect itself, it must hold the criminal justice system accountable.

Punishment

We reluctantly recognize that society will continue (at least for some period) to insist upon punishing some persons for acts which the society designates to be harmful to others. As things stand, this tendency is often converted into a diffuse punitive response toward large "classes" of persons or against a few individuals selected in an arbitrary and discriminating fashion. Moreover, our society has established as

6

CRIME
HAS
SOCIAL ROOTS

No, what the prospective crime commission will tell us, as a long line of previous (and now forgotten) studies have told us is 1) that crime is connected with other social problems and particularly poverty; 2) that crime is principally deterred by the celerity of justice, not the severity of justice; 3) that America's unique, widespread distribution of firearms and particularly handguns is just fine for robbery and murders, and keeps the United States up there at the top of the crime league among all the big nations, and 4) that, if we really want to reduce crime it will cost a pretty penny in social reform and police improvement, and that probably no single investment of money, however big, will so improve the quality of American life as meeting that cost.

TRB, ''Denying the Obvious,'' **The New Republic**, April 12, 1975, p. 2.

crimes many acts which are not actually harmful to others and has failed to respond to other forms of behavior which render serious harm to many citizens. In addition, many forms of punishment have been called by a different name and passed off as non-punitive measures.

We submit that a crime be defined as an act which in some concrete way deprives people of their property, harms them physically, or damages the quality of their lives, and not those acts which merely offend the moral sensibilities of some individuals or groups.

7

Editorial cartoon by Bill Sanders, courtesy of Field Newspaper Syndicate.

We suggest further that it be recognized that any form of restraint or control is punishment. This includes imprisonment, probation, placement in community-based "treatment centers," or forced involvement in any treatment program.

We hold that long periods of, or severe forms of punishment are extremely damaging to those persons being punished and do not deter others from committing criminal offenses; certainty and swiftness, not severity, of punishment has the greatest deterrent effect.

We recommend, therefore, that in operating a system of punishment, the following principles be adhered to:

• Crime must be defined as an act which in some concrete manner deprives a person of his/her property, harms him/her physically, or damages the quality of his/her life. This will entail an extensive rewriting of the law far beyond removing victimless crimes from the statutes.

• The punishment must fit the crime. Characteristics of the individual, individual needs, or other irrelevant criteria must not influence the length or severity of punishment. Shorter flat sentences must be instituted, thus eliminating the indeterminate sentences and the parole system. Maintaining incarceration because it is predicted that the prisoner presents some future danger must also come to an end.

• Punishment must be of short and fixed duration and not exceed two years. The death penalty is unacceptable.

• During periods of restraint, there must be no more loss of rights or freedoms than is necessary to maintain the system of restraint — and only for the period of restraint. Each and every right removed during restraint must be removed by due process. Restraint itself is the sole punishment and there must not be any punishment beyond this. Denial of any rights must be justified on the sole criterion of maintaining the security. The restrained person must be accorded all rights guaranteed the citizen under the Constitution, including, of course, the right to vote.

• Independent boards (comprised, for example, of reppresentatives from the clergy, the bar, academia, other professions, the unions, ex-prisoner groups, and so on who are available to function) must be established to deal with the short-comings and inequities of the system and an independent mechanism to assure just handling of prison grievances (for example, an independent ombudsman organization). We reluctantly recognize that in spite of safeguards provided by legislation and regulations to insure the rights of the arrested and/or the convicted, that those rights continue to be violated. Therefore, constant vigilance must be maintained by the aforementioned groups and citizens to insure that this does not happen and that those responsible for the system are held accountable.

Human Rights

Convicted persons must NOT be considered "things, objects, clients, or possessions." They have the right to be respected as human beings and to be self-determining. These rights must include the following:

• Acceptance or refusal of any program by those convicted must not be the basis of any court decision affecting the length of sentence. Employment within a restraining institution must not be used solely for institutional convenience.

• Medical, vocational-educational services, and so on must be made available on a private sector purchase of service and voluntary basis only.

• A restraining facility or agency should provide the convicted access to services over and above any of those the facility or agency might itself provide.

Correctional Service

It is imperative that the prisoner and ex-prisoner's perspective be incorporated into every aspect of the program-planning, decision-making and implementation within the restraining system. In spite of the social stigma, the ex-prisoner who has been able to function in the community is perhaps in a better position than anyone else to help the prisoner change the direction of his life, to create a new image, a new conscience. Having made the trip the prisoner is on, the ex-prisoner is in touch with what he or she is up against. Because he or she has accomplished a successful transition from prison to community life, the ex-prisoner is a person the prisoner can listen to, speak with, identify with and emulate. The ex-prisoner is in a position to communicate with the prisoner both while in prison and after release and to help change the course of the ex-prisoner's life.

OUR PERMISSIVE SYSTEM OF CRIMINAL JUSTICE

Senator H. L. Richardson

H. L. Richardson is a California state Senator. He made the following speech at the 5th Annual Training Conference of the California Homicide Investigators Association at Sacramento, California.

Consider the following questions while reading:

1. Who does Richardson say are accomplices to the rising crime rates?
2. How are the accomplices encouraging crime?
3. What action to discourage crime does the author suggest?
4. How do you interpret the cartoons in this reading?

Senator H. L. Richardson, "Time to Reaffirm Basic Truths About Crime," **Human Events**, August 31, 1974, pp. 18, 19. Reprinted with permission.

Violence is no longer the manufactured melodrama of the theatrical arts. It has become part of our everyday life — gruesome tragedies, perpetrated against our next-door neighbor, our family and our friends, personally touching each of us. Mathematically, one out of every five families will have a major crime committed against some member of that family.

Crime is the product of flesh and blood individuals — individuals who choose to satisfy their carnal, fiscal and physical desires by denying the rights of others...individuals who willfully choose to assault the person or take over the property of other human beings.

Aided, I might add, by accomplices. Accomplices who have contributed to the rise in crime. These friends of the felon are the professional apologists, the excuse makers, the contemporary environmentalists, the behaviorists...these people who are more interested in bleeding hearts than bleeding victims. They are the ones who blame everybody and everything, except the responsible individual. They blame the ghetto, the lack of education, lack of job opportunity, prejudice, the Deep South, the two-faced North, race, religion, the Establishment, the profit system of our free market, etc., etc.

Society is to blame, is their theme.

This is the same sick theme promoted by those who kidnapped Patty Hearst.

Those behaviorists look to government as their vehicle to remold human behavior...rehabilitation is the total vehicle, punishment is dismissed as archaic. This theme caught hold in the late 30's, and systematically and effectively the purveyors of this new social gospel burrowed their way into correctional departments during the past 40 years. They are now the dominant voice that is heard in probation, parole and our prisons.

Simplistically stated, this is what we hear: ''The total answer is rehabilitation. Incarceration does not work. The anti-social offense has been committed and there is nothing to be done to correct it, so our job now is to readjust, rehabilitate and remold the perpetrator of the act. Punishment is vengeance, thusly it is bad.''

We, who are successfully part of our present day society, have contributed to his violent act and justifiably it is we who should share the blame. **We** are the guilty.

It is easy to see how the next step is rationalized by the criminal to justify his violent acts. Robbery, rape, murder — all become moral acts against an immoral and necessary revolutionary act. Stealing has become no more than a rip-off from an exploiting ''big business community.'' Kidnapping is an act of war to liberate ''political prisoners.''

MONKEY ON UNCLE SAM'S BACK

Reprinted by permission of **The Plain Truth**.

False premises abound in this fuzzy thinking, such as (1) "The criminal **wants** to be rehabilitated and he really wants to work;" (2) "The criminal is sorry for the offense he has committed;" and (3) "He is not really responsible for his acts because our selfish, profit-minded society exploits the poor."

Advocates of this philosophy reside in the present Department of Corrections, including its Division of Parole, and also within the probation departments of our counties. It is taught in our universities and colleges as modern penology and promoted as fact, not theory. This social philosophy is especially attractive to those who dislike the competition of the American way of life — the kind of life where a man is responsible for his own actions. The concept that man controls his own destiny and is accountable is anathema to the Socialist mind.

One point that apologists rarely explain away is why, for every criminal who comes from a slum area, are there thousands from the same area who hold jobs? Why, for every under-educated criminal, are there thousands of successful individuals who made it with less education? Why, for every unemployed criminal, are there thousands who never had to resort to crime as a means of survival?

I was raised in a factory town on the south side of Chicago. A tough neighborhood, what some would call an economically deprived area by today's standards. I dropped out of high school after only two years and joined the Navy to fight for my country in the Second World War. I also came from a broken home. So, I was a high school drop-out, from an economically deprived area and a broken home. I must assume that all those with the same background will grow up to be senators.

It isn't society nor environment that commits crimes. Criminals commit crimes...individuals. Criminal individuals commit crimes.

Once a criminal knew he was committing wrong against society. Now he has been given an excuse for his behavior. The more he is given justification for his acts against society, the more the crime rate will increase. The more we hold men accountable for their acts, no matter who they are, the more peace will prevail.

14

Accountability implies punishment for wrong-doing, but punishment is no longer part of our criminal justice system. The virus that has carried this epidemic of crime into the bowels of America is called socialism. Its concepts permeate the departments of sociology, the social sciences and social work. Is it any wonder that contemporary social concepts dominate the behavioral sciences as they relate to the imprisonment of the criminal element?...

REAL GUN CONTROL

Editorial cartoon by Don Hesse Copyright, **St. Louis Globe-Democrat**, reprinted with permission of Los Angeles Times Syndicate.

Please don't think that I don't believe in certain forms of rehabilitation. I do. The first offender should be given a chance to learn a trade. Second offenders in some cases. Educational opportunities should be provided for those who have less than a high school education. But under **all** circumstances, rehabilitation must be earned by the inmate by industrious work within the institution. All California prisoners should be putting in a 48-hour week. The work ethic is a definite part of rehabilitation....

We should not condone bestiality on the grounds that the offender is the victim of circumstances. The thug who bludgeons an old man to death for $15 in his pocket may be the "victim" of a broken home, but it makes him no less a thug. The age-old cause of crime is still the desire for easy money, greed, passion and cruelty.

CRIME MUST BE PUNISHED

If we mean business about reducing crime, let us accept the elementary usefulness of a prison as a place of imprisonment. The reformers are fond of saying that it "does no good" to put a man behind bars for 10 to 15 years, at least, the criminal is out of circulation. He is not robbing, assaulting, raping, killing or stealing. Incarceration has its manifest virtues. Let us be just; let us be humane; let us persist in rehabilitative efforts for the 10 or 20 per cent who may in fact be turned around; but let us abandon the soft euphemism of "correction," and think in terms of punishment and isolation instead.

James J. Kilpatrick, "The Way to Reduce Crime," **Nation's Business**, April, 1975, p. 8.

The maudlin attitude of renunciation of "legal revenge" has been proven wrong since the beginning of time. The present crime rate proves it is wrong. It is an extravagant and dangerous belief that terrorists and habitual spoilers can be changed into new men by soft justice, short sentences, liberal parole and trust. Approximately 47 per cent of the graduates of what we mistakenly call our "criminal justice system" are back in custody on further offenses within three years, and usually for more serious crimes.

In 1968, the Supreme Court of Utah stated, "The prime requisite towards a good relationship between the prisoner and his rehabilitation is his acknowledgement and acceptance of the fact that he has done wrong, and the realization that society is his benefactor, trying to improve his lot so he can become a useful citizen. It is difficult to supervise a man who is looking for loopholes through which he can escape from the results of his criminal tendencies. Each time he is let out on a technicality, he believes the court is on his side and he does not have to conform to any standards, except those which he sets for himself."

The inter-relationship between the new liberalism and the rocketing crime rate is too consistent to be waived aside. All laws are founded on the premise that there is wickedness in the world. And they are intended to act as a barrier between right and wrong....

It is long past time to reaffirm some basic truths: It is morally wrong to steal, to lie and to cheat. It is evil to willfully harm another human. It is a sin to murder and it is sinful when you don't hold a man accountable for his actions. Civilization and human society can only exist when those who destroy the citizen's individual rights are quickly and effectively punished. Are we to be crushed by contemporary barbarians?

I believe we deserve a better fate.

Common sense has long been one of America's antidotes to its ills — personal accountability is another. I suggest we take a large dose of both.

DISTINGUISHING PRIMARY FROM SECONDARY SOURCES

A critical thinker must always question his various sources of information. Historians, for example, usually distinguish between **primary sources** (eyewitness accounts) and **secondary sources** (writings based on primary or eyewitness accounts, or other secondary sources.) A diary written by a Civil War veteran is one example of a primary source. In order to be a critical reader one must be able to recognize primary sources. However, this is not enough. Eyewitness accounts do not always provide accurate descriptions. Historians may find ten different eyewitness accounts of an event and all the accounts might interpret the event differently. Then they must decide which of these accounts provide the most objective and accurate interpretations.

Test your skill in evaluating sources by participating in the following exercise. Pretend you are living 2000 years in the future. Your teacher tells you to write an essay about the causes of the Watergate scandals during the Nixon Administration. Richard M. Nixon served as president from his inauguration in 1969 to the day he resigned on August 9, 1974. Consider carefully each of the following source descriptions. First, **underline** only those descriptions you feel would serve as a primary source for your essay. Second, **rank** only the underlined or primary sources assigning the number (1) to the most objective and accurate primary source, number (2) to the next most accurate and so on until the ranking is finished. Then discuss and compare your evaluations with other class members.

Assume that all of the following sources deal with the broad topic of the Watergate scandal and its causes.

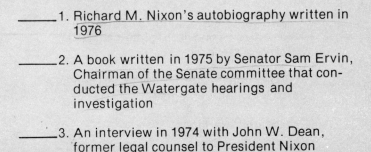

_____1. Richard M. Nixon's autobiography written in 1976

_____2. A book written in 1975 by Senator Sam Ervin, Chairman of the Senate committee that conducted the Watergate hearings and investigation

_____3. An interview in 1974 with John W. Dean, former legal counsel to President Nixon

_____ 4. A speech by Premier Fidel Castro of Cuba in 1975

_____ 5. A newspaper editorial written in 1974 by Maurice Stans, former finance chairman of the committee to reelect President Nixon

_____ 6. A book published in 1980 written by an American political scientist of conservative political persuasion

_____ 7. A book published in 1978 written by a Brazilian sociologist who had never traveled to the U.S.

_____ 8. A book published in 1979 written by an American political scientist of liberal political persuasion

_____ 9. A speech in 1975 by Senator George McGovern

_____ 10. A book published in 1976 written by a Canadian political scientist specializing in American political life

_____ 11. An essay by President Ford written in 1982

_____ 12. A book published in 1975 written by Bernstein and Woodward, the two journalists from the **Washington Post** newspaper who were primarily responsible for exposing the Watergate scandals

_____ 13. An interview in 1976 with Judge John Sirica who presided over the Watergate trials

_____ 14. A newspaper editorial in 1973 by John Mitchell who served as one of President Nixon's Attorneys General

_____ 15. A book published in 2857 A.D. written by a Japanese anthropologist

_____ 16. The Watergate tapes

_____ 17. The televised Senate Watergate hearings

BLACKS VICTIMIZED BY HARSH LEGAL TREATMENT

Viewpoint Newsletter

Viewpoint newsletter is published by the Foundation for Change, Inc. **Viewpoint** attempts to document the minority outlook and is aimed at white students whose contact with minority attitudes may be limited. **Viewpoint** is offered to all students and teachers who want material on racism.

Use the following questions to assist you while reading:

1. According to **Viewpoint**, how does our criminal justice system discriminate against black people?
2. What is the effect of legal racism on blacks?
3. How do you interpret the cartoon in this reading?

"Justice Stands Trial for Racism," **Viewpoint** #4, June, 1971.

Who Is Justice? I would like to know,
Whoever she is, I could love her so.
I could love her, though my race
So seldom looks upon her face.

— John Henrik Clarke, **Harlem Stirs**, 1966.

Justice is supposed to be color-blind. The U.S. Constitution entitles all citizens to equal protection of the law. But the President's Advisory Council on Civil Disorders (1968 Kerner Commission) found that the poor and the Black don't trust ''The Man's law.'' The Commission reported that from ''arrest to sentencing the poor are denied equal justice.'' Ghetto witnesses charged that the court's bail system keeps them in jail before trial, while the rich buy their freedom to prepare their cases.

The Kerner Report and other studies made these points:

• Blacks are disproportionately arrested on suspicion compared to whites.

• Non-whites receive longer sentences than whites for the same offenses.

• More than one-third of all those in prison are black.

• Blacks are less likely than whites to serve on juries, but more likely to be convicted by juries.

• The poor and the Black have been the chief victims of the death penalty.

• Violent crime is **intra-racial**: Blacks are most often victims of Black offenders while whites are most often victimized by whites.

BAIL OR JAIL

Blacks are 75% of prisoners in big city jails. Of these, more than half are awaiting trial, some for over a year, even though they have not been convicted of an offense. Their crime is that they do not have the price of their temporary release — bail money. Most do not have the price of a lawyer, either. A Black ex-prisoner recently told a CBS television audience: ''The brothers

WHY DO I HAVE
TO BE YOUR HANG-UP?

Reprinted by permission of the **Chicago Defender**.

who are too poor to afford a lawyer get Legal Aid. They don't ask them whether they're guilty. They tell them what plea they can get.''

Courts call this ''plea bargaining'': the defendant gets a reduced sentence if he agrees to waive trial and plead guilty. The justification is that it eases the court case load. In fact, in 9 out of 10 criminal cases there is no trial.

UNEQUAL JUSTICE

Over 3,000 Negroes have been lynched during past years in this country, about 350 unarmed Negroes murdered in the last decade, and so far not one white man has been executed for any of these murders and almost none convicted, according to Dr. Leroy D. Clark, professor of law at New York University.

Charles A. Wells, **Between the Lines**, October 1, 1970, p. 1.

LEGAL RACISM

Justice today bears the scars of legal racism that began with slave codes and continued with laws that discriminated against free Blacks, too, in the North as well as the South. For example: Blacks could not serve on juries, bring lawsuits or testify against white men. One carry-over of such racist laws has been to exclude most Blacks from the legal process except as defendants. The U.S. Commission on Civil Rights reports that government law agencies across the country have almost no minorities on staff. Until recently, Blacks were barred from most law schools and lawyers' associations in the South. North and South, Blacks are less than 2% of all lawyers. They are still kept off many juries by a selection system that favors middle-class occupations and middle-class neighborhoods.

Former Supreme Court Justice Earl Warren asks: **"How long can we expect the Black people of our country to respect the law and its processes if their rights are denied?"**

Non-whites charge that the only time they are noticed by the law is when they break it. Judges, district attorneys and juries are usually whites. Federal judges are appointed for life by the President. Local judges are appointed by governors and mayors, or elected on political party tickets. These judges appoint jury commissioners who set up jury lists. Blacks, more than 11% of our population, are under-represented in our court system and over-represented in punishment.

24

JUDGES, a national picture:

- there are 278 Black judges in the U.S. — under 2% of total.
- of about 700 federal judges, 20 are Black. South has none.
- of 16,000 full-time state judges, only 258 are Black.

One Black man has made it to the Supreme Court: Thurgood Marshall. One Black woman has been picked for a federal judgeship: Constance Baker Motley.

LAWYERS, a national picture:

- of 93 United States Attorneys, none is Black.
- of 325,000 lawyers, 4,000 are Black — under 2%.
- about 50 Puerto Rican lawyers serve 1.5 million Puerto Ricans in the U.S.

JURIES: The NAACP Legal Defense and Education Fund has brought several cases to the Supreme Court on the grounds that a selection system excludes Blacks from the jury box, thereby depriving Black defendants of the right to be judged by a jury of their peers (equals). The law says that juries must be taken from voter registration lists and represent a fair cross-section of the community. But in Philadelphia, where prospective jurors are interviewed, present jury panels are reported to have one-third more whites than their share of the city's population and one-third fewer Blacks. Here are some recent statistics pointing to bias in Metropolitan New York

In Manhattan (1965-1967):

- 1.1 out of every 10,000 Harlem voters were on the grand jury list, but —
- 62.2 out of every 10,000 white voters from the upper income East Side were on the grand jury list.

In The Bronx (1967):
- of 17% Black population, 8% were grand jurors.
- of 21% Puerto Ricans, 1.1% were on the grand jury.

SENTENCING, of inmates sentenced to Federal prisons in fiscal 1970:

	Whites	Non-Whites
Average Sentence	42.9 months	57.5 months
Income Tax Evasion	12.8 months	28.6 months
Drug Cases	61.1 months	81.1 months

CAPITAL PUNISHMENT: Here is how the Federal Bureau of Prisons breaks down the death toll from 1930 to 1967, when executions were suspended pending U.S. Supreme Court decisions on death sentence cases.

Overall Death Penalty: 2,066 Blacks (53.5%), 42 from other races, and 1,751 whites have been put to death.

Death Penalty for Murder: 1,630 Blacks, 40 from other races, and 1,664 whites were executed.

Death Penalty for Robbery and Burglary: 36 people were executed. 30 were Black.

Death Penalty for Rape: Although over half of all convicted rapists are white, of the 455 men executed only 48 were white. 405 Blacks died along with 2 from other races.

STIFFER PENALTIES NEEDED FOR BLACK OFFENDERS

Allan C. Brownfeld

Allan C. Brownfield is a free lance writer and lecturer. Among the conservative publications he has contributed to are **Human Events**, **The Phoenix Gazette** and **The Manchester Union Leader**.

The following questions should help you understand the reading:

1. Who does the author say is responsible for crime?
2. What does he say black leaders want done about crime?
3. Why does he claim black leaders are concerned about crime?
4. How does the cartoon in this reading support the author's ideas?

Allan C. Brownfeld, "Black Leaders Decry Crime and Lax Law Enforcement," **Human Events**, February 1, 1975, p. 8. Reprinted with permission.

Advocates of the notion that "society" rather than the individual criminal is responsible for crime, or of the idea that "punishment" is an old-fashioned and barbaric concept, and should be replaced with more lenient and "humane" methods of law enforcement, were surprised and shocked at the recent annual meeting of the National League of Cities, held in Houston, Tex., in December 1974.

The reason for their shock and surprise was that the very group to whom they sought to appeal with such a "soft" view of the nation's mounting crime and violence — black mayors, councilmen, county commissioners and judges — were of an entirely different point of view. These black officials were concerned not primarily with the interests of the criminal but, far more important, with the interests of law-abiding citizens who fear to leave their homes, to walk the streets, or to send their children to school.

One of the most crowded workshops at the Houston meeting concerned "Minority Groups and the Criminal Justice System."

The workshop participants, who were mostly black, spent most of their time arguing that poverty, illiteracy, poor health, and idleness were the main engines of crime in ethnic slum areas and that society's ills must be treated if there is to be hope that crime will be controlled.

Then, during the discussion period, the audience took an entirely different and much firmer approach. A city councilman from Gary, Ind., said: "I don't blame social problems for crime" and then criticized the city's local courts as "criminal release machines."

A black councilman from Knoxville, Tenn., argued against such violence-producing movies as **Superfly** as well as "lighter sentences for black criminals apprehended in poor black communities" than those apprehended elsewhere. Such "leniency," meant by white liberals to show their concern for past prejudice, only exacerbates the situation, he stated.

Judge Andrew Jefferson, a member of the Houston Court of Domestic Relations, criticized the "two or three-time syndrome," where troublesome youths tend to get several reprieves from schools, the juvenile authorities, and courts before finally being called to account.

Ben Holman, director of the Justice Department's Community Relations Service, who was also a panelist, said in an interview that there was a new anxiety among blacks about crime and that he had been summoned to city after city to be asked his advice on meeting the crime problem.

Editorial cartoon by Don Hesse Copyright, **St. Louis Globe-Democrat**, reprinted with permission of Los Angeles Times Syndicate.

Mr. Holman said that he told community groups to press their local leaders to use revenue-sharing funds for broader purposes than simply the purchase of equipment. He suggested that some of the federal money be given to black community groups that have their own anti-crime projects.

The concern of the overwhelming majority of black Americans with the rising crime rate — which reaches its height within predominantly black innercity areas — should come as no surprise. The concept that black Americans either hate or fear the police is one which the media has spent much time in developing but which, in fact, has little basis in reality. That this should be true, in light of very real instances of brutality aimed at blacks in the past by many police departments, is particularly revealing.

At the height of racial tension which plagued the nation in the mid-60's, shortly after riots in Watts and in Harlem, polls were taken within the black community of both areas. The poll conducted in Watts by John F. Kraft, Inc., an independent public opinion research organization, showed that the majority of blacks sympathized with police problems and wanted more instead of fewer policemen in their neighborhood.

Similarly, in Harlem the people expressed the view that the worst problems facing their community, in this order, were the following: narcotics addiction, 21 per cent; crime and juvenile delinquency, 11 per cent; the need for better schools, 11 per cent; the breakdown of family life, 10 per cent.

"Problems of police brutality are conspicuous by their absence," the Kraft report said. "It appears that police malpractice in Harlem is an issue only insofar as the police are inadequate in doing their jobs."

Black groups throughout the country have been active in the anti-crime fight. One which has been particularly effective is Any Boy Can (ABC), founded by former light heavyweight champion Archie Moore. The group takes boys who are either juvenile delinquents or headed in that direction, and the underprivileged, and helps them find a life of responsibility and respect.

Moore declares that "The devil is at work in America, and it is up to us to drive him out. Snipers, looters, white or black, deserve no mercy. Those who would profit from their brother's misfortunes deserve no mercy, and those who would set fellow Americans upon each other deserve no mercy."

RECYCLING DANGEROUS CRIMINALS

Now what this means is that we are in effect recycling dangerous criminals, through the police, through the courts, and back out onto the street without their being kept out of circulation. So of more than half of the very violent-type crimes and crimes that cause a great deal of fear, more than half the people that we have to deal with are people we've already handled. People who if they had been kept out of circulation would not be victimizing additional citizens. Now this percentage was much less 10 years ago.

Statement by Los Angeles Police Chief Edward M. Davis excerpted from "Tough Words on Crime by L.A. Police Chief," **Human Events**, March 22, 1975, p. 248.

When white Americans who claim to be "sophisticated" speak in a patronizing manner about black crime, they are in the opposite corner of the arena from most black Americans. The blacks were represented by those officials in Houston who want more, and not less, law enforcement.

DISTINGUISHING BIAS FROM REASON

One of the most important critical thinking skills is the ability to distinguish between opinions based on emotions or bias and conclusions based on a rational consideration of **facts**. This discussion exercise is designed to promote experimentation with one's capacity to recognize **biased** statements.

Some of the following statements have been taken from the readings in this chapter and some have other origins. Consider each statement carefully. Mark (**R**) for any statement you feel is based on a rational consideration of the facts. Mark (**P**) for any statement you believe is based on prejudice or emotion. Mark (**I**) for any statement you think is impossible to judge. Then discuss and compare your judgments with other class members.

R = REASON
P = PREJUDICE
I = IMPOSSIBLE TO JUDGE

_____ 1. Indians in America are a colonized people.

_____ 2. Black people are remarkable entertainers.

_____ 3. Civilization can only exist when crime is effectively punished.

_____ 4. Convicted persons must be rehabilitated not punished.

_____ 5. Indians are mainly skilled at hunting and fishing.

_____ 6. The pardon of Richard Nixon violates the principle of equal justice under the law.

_____ 7. It is an extravagant and dangerous belief that terrorists and habitual spoilers can be changed into new men by soft justice, short sentences, liberal parole and trust.

_____ 8. In every society racial values are as important as other values.

_____ 9. Minorities in America today have greater opportunities than in past years.

_____10. Black people are a significant cause of the increasing crime rate in American cities.

_____11. The death penalty is unacceptable.

_____12. The most important aspect of any nation is its racial heritage.

_____13. Poor people generally lack initiative and creativity.

_____14. Integration could destroy racial identity and individuality.

_____15. The energy crisis has helped to inflate the economy.

_____16. In America inflation has had a devastating impact on minorities and the poor.

2 CHAPTER

ECONOMIC JUSTICE

CAPITALISM EQUALS ECONOMIC INJUSTICE

Eugene Toland, Thomas Fenton, & Lawrence McCulloch, M. M.

Eugene Toland, Thomas Fenton, and Lawrence McCulloch are Maryknoll priests. The Catholic Maryknoll Order is an organization of priests, brothers, and nuns who work in foreign missions.

Reflect on the following questions while you read:

1. What three myths about capitalism do the authors claim exist in America?
2. What do they say about the distribution of wealth in the U.S.?
3. Do the authors suggest an alternative to capitalism?
4. How do you interpret the cartoons in this reading?

Eugene Toland, Thomas Fenton, and Lawrence McCulloch, ''World Justice And Peace: A Radical Analysis For American Christians.''

This paper contends that the system which creates and sustains much of the hunger, underdevelopment, unemployment and other social ills in the world today is **capitalism**. Capitalism is by its very nature a system which promotes individualism, competition and profit-making with little or no regard for the social cost. It places profits and private gain before social services and human needs. As such it is an unjust system which should be replaced....

In this paper we will respond to certain myths about capitalism... These are myths that are rarely articulated, much less challenged, in many of our church discussions on world justice and peace....

Capitalism and the Distribution of Wealth in the U.S.

Myth No. 1: Reforms of the capitalist system within the United States have brought about a more equitable distribution of wealth and power among our people than ever before.

Fact: The distribution of wealth in the U.S. is almost identical with the distribution of wealth in India.[1] The only difference is that in the U.S. the economic pie is much bigger and so the results of this maldistribution are not quite as visible. Furthermore, with this wealth goes much of the control over the country's resources, industry, and public services.

In 1941, ⅔ of all manufacturing assets in the nation were controlled by 1,000 large corporations.[2] Today a mere 200 giant corporations control this same percentage, i.e., a cool $350 billion.[3] Despite the claim of "people's capitalism," these corporations are owned by less than 2% of the American population. According to the Lampman report, published in 1962, 80% of all corporate stock was owned by the top 1.6% of the population, or 1.5 million people. Even more, the richest of the rich, the top 5% of this upper 1.6%, owned half of this group's stocks. Thus 75,000 people, each with assets of $500,000 or more, owned at least 40% of all corporate stock in the country.[4]

Not only is the wealth of the nation, i.e., the factories, utilities, banks, etc., largely owned by a very small percentage of the population, but the yearly national income is equally maldistributed. According to a recent Brookings Institute study conducted by economist Joseph Pechman, the lowest fifth of American families receives only 3.2% of the national income while the highest fifth gets 45.8%, or more than fourteen times as much. Moreover, according to this study, the top 1% of American families receive more than twice the income of the 20% who occupy the bottom rung of the U.S. income ladder. [5]

LAUREL & HARDY

Andrews in **The Daily World**, reprinted by permission.

An even more revealing way to look at the economy is through the influence and control which a mere handful of multi-billionaire families and financial groups have exerted for generations. The Rockefeller empire is not a thing of the past. Neither are the Dupont or Mellon trusts relics of another age....

Capitalism and Poltical Power in the U.S.

Myth No. 2: Despite the concentration of wealth in our country, we can trust in a democratically elected government to work for the welfare of all the people.

Fact: The small elite that runs our economy also dominates political life, especially at the federal level, making radical and far-reaching social reform almost impossible. Most members of the legislative and executive branches of the U.S. government are drawn from this financial elite and from the lawyers and economists who work for it. During the 90th Congress, the House of Representatives alone had 97 bankers, twelve of whom served on the House Banking Commission. [6]

One way this group uses its political influence to maintain and even increase its slice of the national wealth is through its manipulation of the tax structure. Despite claims of ''progressive taxation,'' the rich and super-rich have consistently provided themselves with legal gimmicks and loopholes to protect their huge fortunes. The result is that the burden of ever higher, more unjust taxes increasingly falls onto the backs of lower and middle income families.

These gimmicks and loopholes are well known: oil depletion allowances, tax exempt bonds, capital gains write-offs, executive expense accounts, farm subsidies, stock options, etc. Avoiding taxes and growing fat at the federal trough is itself a big business. Here are a few examples:

In 1967, 21 millionaires paid no federal taxes at all. [7] In 1968, 155 persons with incomes exceeding $200 thousand paid no taxes. [8] From 1913 to the present the Rockefellers have paid less than $17 million in inheritance taxes on a fortune estimated at from $3 to $5 billion. [9]

In 1964, the Atlantic Oil Co. paid no taxes on its

earnings of $410 million.[10] In 1962, Standard Oil of N.J. which has a greater income than most countries in the world, paid out only .6% of its staggering profits to the IRS.[11]

In 1963, the upper 1.6% of the population owned all municipal and state tax exempt bonds, worth $85.9 billion. These bonds provide for the very rich $2.5 billion of untaxed income every year.[12]

In 1966, $250 million in farm subsidies was paid to .02% of the population of Texas while 28% of the people living below the poverty line received less than $7 million in all forms of food assistance.[13] In 1968, a single farm in California, the J. G. Boswell Co., received over $3 million in subsidies[14] and the enormously wealthy Hawaiian Commercial and Sugar Co. got a fat $1.2 million for not growing pineapples.[15]

"WE PLAY NO FAVORITES...
EVERYONE PAYS
THROUGH THE SAME FUNNEL."

Palmer in the **Springfield Leader-Press**, reprinted by permission.

These are but a few examples. They should help remind us that what we are dealing with in the United States, as Justice Douglas has said, is a system of socialism for the rich and "free enterprise" for the poor....[16]

Capitalism and Patriotism

Myth No. 3: To attack capitalism is anti-American; it is to attack the system that has made this country great.

Fact: To attack capitalism is not anti-American for the simple reason that, as we have seen above, most Americans are not capitalists. The fact that, in a trillion dollar economy, we still have over thirty million Americans living in poverty, and millions more with no real financial security (i.e. mortgages on homes, etc.) is striking proof that our economy is owned by and for a very small elite.

As Americans we are rightfully proud of our democratic traditions, traditions that uphold the rights of every individual to free speech, freedom of assembly, freedom of religion, etc. We believe in a government of the people, by the people and for the people. We are opposed, as Jefferson said, "to any form of tyranny over the mind of man." As a people, we agree that democracy, while maybe not the neatest and most efficient way to run a country, is still the best.

Because of this pride in American democracy, however, when we approach issues of justice and peace we have a difficult time distinguishing democracy from capitalism. Democracy, after all, is a **political** system. It is a system where people vote for candidates who will represent them in government and rule them for a limited period of time. Capitalism, however, is an **economic** system where, for example, one individual owns a factory and hires others to work in it. While few people would deny that democracy is a good thing, capitalism is the opposite of democracy, since it is an economic system not owned by the people and run for the people, but a system owned and run by a plutocracy, i.e., the rich and super-rich.

Neither can we say that it is capitalism that has produced such great wealth in the United States. Those who have produced the wealth are the workers, blacks and whites, Greeks, Irish, Polish, and Chicano, generation after generation of hard-working men and

40

"U.S. Says Rich Get Biggest Tax Breaks," **Minneapolis Tribune**, May 27, 1975, p. 3A.

women. And it is precisely these people, the working people of all races and creeds and nationalities, who have made America great, who must constantly struggle even to gain a minimal share in the wealth they have produced, as if it did not belong to them in the first place.

A phrase we hear a lot about today is "community control." In many respects this would represent the best in American democracy. Only when the people, both urban and rural, own their own land, their own factories, their own schools, their own banks, their own hospitals, and their own means of protection and law enforcement, will the vision of a truly democratic America become a reality. In many respects, this is a modern day version of Jeffersonian democracy: a country made up of artisans and family farmers, each person owning a part of the assets of this great land and sharing equally in the fruits of his own labor.

But the direction of the American economy today is just the opposite. Each year a quarter of a million family farmers leave their land[17] because they can no longer compete with the huge corporate agri-businesses that are gobbling up the countryside and dominating the purchasing and distribution of farm produce. Each year thousands of small businessmen close shop because they can no longer compete with the chain stores that undercut and outlast them. Each year hundreds of even medium and large companies are bought out and added to the growing list of subsidiaries of the huge conglomerates.

No, speaking against capitalism is not speaking against what has made this country great. The people have made this country great and they deserve full democratic control over the economic as well as political aspects of their life.

Conclusion

We have looked, then, at some of the myths which prevent us from seeing clearly the nature of capitalism and how it really works....

With these myths gone we can better see the roots of many of the injustices which face us today. Bloated stomachs, refugees, chronic unemployment, crowded urban ghettos, rising taxes, the breakdown of social services to the aged, the handicapped, the imprisoned, the lack of money for schools, hospitals, mass transit, and the continuance of imperialistic wars, etc. are all products of a system — a system which reaps excess for the few and scatters crumbs for the many.

As men and women thirsting for justice we are naive if we fail to take a hard, critical look at this system. If we do not do our homework, we might jump to the false conclusion that it is the average working man, the average parishoner, the average white suburbanite who is the culprit. We are more on the mark if we recognize that a common characteristic of the white worker, most women, Chicanos, blacks, farmers, Indians, office workers, etc., be they here in the U.S. or in other countries, is that they are exploited by the super-rich in a system designed to be unfair.

FOOTNOTES

1 Lundberg, Ferdinand, **The Rich and the Super-Rich**, Bantam Books, 1968, p. 24.
2 **Economic Report on Corporate Mergers**, Bureau of Economics, Federal Trade Commission, Commerce Clearing House Edition, p. 3.
3 **Fortune**, Time Inc., May 1971, pp. 172-178.
4 Lampman, Robert, **The Share of Top Wealth-Holders in Personal Wealth, 1922-1956**, Princeton Univ. Press, Princeton, N.J., pp. 75-80, 97, 208.
5 **Progressive**, Madison, Wisc., February 1972, p. 6.

6 Tanzer, Michael, **The Sick Society**, Holt, Rinehart & Winston, N.Y., 1971, p. 46.
7 Time, April 4, 1969.
8 Joseph Kraft, **Herald Tribune**, International Ed., Feb. 11, 1969.
9 Lundberg, **Rich. and the Super-Rich**, op. cit., p. 185.
10 Gregory, Dick, **No More Lies**, Harper & Row, N.Y., 1971, p. 171.
11 Ibid.
12 Lundberg, **The Rich and the Super-Rich**, op. cit., p. 428.
13 Douglas, William O., **Points of Rebellion**, Vintage Books, 1970, p. 72.
14 N.Y. Times Almanac, op. cit., p. 650.
15 Green, Felix, **The Enemy**, Random House, N.Y. 1970, p. 256.
16 Douglas, **op. cit.**, p. 68.
17 Pocket Data Book, U.S.A., U.S. Dept. of Commerce, 1971, p. 217.

CAPITALISM PROMOTES ECONOMIC FREEDOM

Charles H. Smith, Jr.

Charles H. Smith, Jr. has served as President of the United States Chamber of Commerce and Chairman of the Board of SIFCO Industries, Inc.

As you read try to answer the following questions:

1. How does the author define economic freedom, and what influence does he say this freedom has had on American society?
2. What does he say about economic controls and their effect?
3. Can you relate the cartoon in this reading to the author's idea?

Charles H. Smith, Jr., "Individual Freedom And Liberty," **Vital Speeches**, June 1, 1974, pp. 511, 512. Reprinted with permission.

It is a significant honor that you have bestowed on me by asking that I assume the leadership for one year of the largest, and I believe the finest, most influential business organization in the world.

I feel a little like President Lincoln when one of his supporters expressed the belief that ''God Almighty and Abraham Lincoln are going to save this country.''

Lincoln laughed and said, ''My friend, you're half right.''

The job that must be done is certainly beyond the power of any one man. But that is not an excuse for failing to try.

For with this honor comes a responsibility — a very great and grave responsibility — a responsibility to speak out in a loud and forceful voice in support of the principles that have enabled this glorious nation in the short span of less than two centuries to develop from a savage wilderness into the most advanced civilization, the most equitable society in history; a society providing the highest standard of living to the greatest number of people that this world has ever seen. And all of this has been accomplished while providing an unprecedented degree of individual freedom and liberty.

More correctly, these accomplishments have been attained not **"while providing"** this high level of individual freedom, but instead, **because of providing** maximum liberty and freedom.

Our great economic progress — our high standard of living — came about directly because here every individual has not only the freedom to dream, but more important, the freedom to pursue those dreams; the freedom to identify a need and try to fill it, be it delivering newspapers or building a 200 million dollar refinery. Be it finding a cure for polio, like Jonas Salk, or finding a formula for laughter like Bob Hope or Flip Wilson.

It is the free market place that has proven to be incalculably more efficient than anything else ever devised to allocate resources in a manner that comes closest to fulfilling the needs and desires of the public. Not the elite, but the public.

FAIREST ECONOMIC SYSTEM

Yes, America, even on a full stomach, is in a period of self-doubt. A recent publication of the Boston Consulting Group says, "Our long range interests would be best served if the public understood that our economic system
a) is the fairest as well as the most fruitful in the world,
b) belongs not to the chosen few but to everyone,
c) can adapt to change, and,
d) preserves and promotes the almost limitless freedom of choice in daily living which has been denied to most people."

R. A. Riley, "Three Lights In The Tower," **Vital Speeches**, June 1, 1974, p. 493.

The competition of the free market place far excels the most zealous consumer advocates, the most concerned congressmen, the most dedicated government bureaucrats all put together in advancing the interests of the general public.

And yet today, to a greater degree than ever before, the basic freedoms that have made our nation great are being compromised in a way that could, if not reversed, destroy our free economy long before my grandchildren are old enough to enjoy it.

Senator Barry Goldwater recently told a group, "The competitive enterprise system is now face-to-face with one of the greatest threats in this country's 200 year history. It is under attack by demagogues who would like to nationalize all basic enterprise in this country, and there is a greater chance of their success than at any time in our history."

We've endured almost three years of a disastrous attempt to mask with economic controls the effects of highly inflationary policies organized and pursued by the political leadership of our nation almost continuously for the last three decades. And yet, we don't have to go further than most first semester economics text-

46

books to know that inflation is the inevitable result of government spending in excess of its income over any extended period. There have been only four years since the Korean War when our Federal Government has operated in the black, with a total net deficit of 143 billion dollars for that period. Is it any wonder that we have inflation?

THE TOWERING INFERNO

Reprinted by permission of **The Indianapolis News**.

We've endured more than three decades of a steadily strengthening alliance between politicians — anxious to insure their own re-election at any price — and labor union leaders who are anxious to maintain or enhance the unbridled monopoly power that gives them such tremendous leverage on the pocket books of the American public. And yet our nation learned over three-quarters of a century ago that monopoly in any form must be eliminated or regulated if we are to have a sound and equitable economy.

We've endured a whole series of attacks on American business by certain "elitist" elements of the news media.

Many commentators are motivated by a sincere desire to improve a good, though imperfect system; but a few of them are evidently motivated by a desire to destroy the economic system that created them, and many more are trapped by the misguided belief that it sells more newspapers and magazines — or gains more viewers — to attack and vilify business than it does to balance the criticism; the belief that a subject is only newsworthy if it is sensationalistic and frightening.

We've endured a whole series of attacks on American business by politicians here in Washington and scattered across our nation in state houses and city councils; politicians who pretend to represent the people while actually victimizing them. Their answer to any problem is government regulation, and the failure of regulation they would rectify with still more regulation.

These politicians have for too long ignored the wisdom of Thomas Jefferson who once said, "Were we directed from Washington when to sow, and when to reap, we should soon want for bread."

If Jefferson were alive today, he might say: "When we're directed from Washington where to build pipelines and how to mine coal, we should soon want for energy."

A newspaper in Kansas — the **Caney Chronicle** — summed it all up nicely in an editorial on the demagogery of the Senate oil industry hearings.

The **Chronicle** had this to say to the Senators:

"You're looking down your noses at the most successful of America's business executives. Take a good look, because they represent the interfiber of our nation.

"They're no different from the small town merchant, the Kansas farmer, the insurance man, the barber or the TV repairman.

"They use good management techniques, hire expert workers, make fine products, maintain good profits...and, balance their books.

"They're successful.

"Now let's take an honest look at you, gentlemen:

"You were hired by the American people to run a business, too. And it may be "hokey" to say, but you've made a dandy mess of things in your job.

"You've raised your own wages by 400 percent in the past fifteen years. You've consistently overspent your budget. You've hired incompetent people, you've overstaffed every government building in the nation. You ridicule your company's top management. You refuse to cooperate with the other departments in your company. You devalue your product at every opportunity.

"At times, gentlemen, you've given encouragement to your chief competitor.

"Perhaps we're wrong, but it seems that you could take some lessons from those 'profit-hungry tycoons who cheat the American people.'

"If anyone should be lining up a panel of men to use as a verbal shooting gallery, it should be the businessmen of America...and you, gentlemen, should answer the questions."

That's the **Caney Chronicle**. I wish we had a lot more like it.

Reminds me of an occasion back when Edward Everett Hale was Chaplain of the Senate. Someone asked him, "Do you pray for the Senators, Dr. Hale?"

He said, "No, I look at the Senators and pray for the country."

Well, I guess the problem has its humorous side. But all-in-all, it's a pretty gloomy picture.

And yet I do not believe that this is a time for despair.

I have not the slightest doubt that if the people are given the truth — the real picture about the role of business in providing jobs and the goods and services we all want and need; about the relationship between investment and jobs; about the relationship between profits and investment; about the relative proportions of wages, and profits, and taxes in our American economy; about the relationship between excessive government spending and inflation; about the relationship between union monopoly power and violence in the construction industry and the high cost of housing — if all of these things, and many more are clearly presented to the American people, I have no doubt that the people will make the right decisions.

But time is running out! The American people are **not** getting the true story, and the situation grows daily more dangerous for the survival of the free market, and more important, for freedom itself, because the two are inseparable. The time has come for every individual who believes in our economic system to rise up in wrath and indignation and say to our Congress: "STOP! We've had enough! It is time to get back to sound economic principles:

I can call on each of you, as you return to your homes and business all over America, to pledge to devote a significant part of your time and your personal effort to get the true story of American business known and understood across the face of our great land. And when I say **your personal** time and effort that is exactly what I mean! We must each personally get involved in getting the business message to the public, to our friends, to our employees, and shareholders, and most important, to our legislators, congressmen, and government officials.

I pledge to you that during the year ahead the Chamber of Commerce of the United States will be in the forefront of such an effort. If we will each put our hearts, our energy, indeed our sacred honor into it, I am confident in the future of America.

50

CHALLENGING CORPORATE MONOPOLY

Jeremy Rifkin

Jeremy Rifkin has been a coordinator of the Citizens Commission of Inquiry on U.S. War Crimes and the Peoples American Revolutionary Bi-Centennial Commission. He delivered the following speech before a Bicentennial conference of over 300 corporate executives. What follows is an edited version of his speech.

Consider the following questions while reading:

1. How does the author say corporations are guilty of treason?
2. What does he say about the public opinion polls?
3. Why does he believe the corporations are Tories?
4. How does the cartoon in this reading support the author's ideas?

Reprinted from a speech by Jeremy Rifkin, "The Bicentennial of What?" and distributed by the Peoples Bicentennial Commission.

The sponsors of this conference have told me that I could not use the word "treason" on a public platform in relation to corporate America, unless I could back up my allegation with facts. I think that is a fair thing to ask. I think we ought to examine the allegation of treason very closely, for if the giant corporations really are subverting the Constitution, the Declaration of Independence, and the Bill of Rights, if they are subverting all the values we believe in, then we certainly would not want them to participate in the Bicentennial of a Revolution. That would be as ludicrous as George Washington inviting Benedict Arnold to the victory celebration at Yorktown.

Have the corporations subverted the Constitution of the United States and the principles of government of, by and for the people? It is an ancient maxim of power — and I'm sure the corporate representatives in this room know this ancient maxim all too well — that whoever controls the economic wealth of a country controls its political decisions. That is a maxim that has held true throughout recorded history. Today 200 giant corporations control ⅔ of the manufacturing assets of the United States of America. Of the hundred largest money powers in the world today 36 of them are not even countries anymore. They are American corporations. We have these giant nations within the nation. These corporate institutions control vast amounts of resources, people and property. So while it is interesting to talk about the private sector vs. the public sector, we all know in reality that such distinctions do not exist any more. The '72 elections have shown us that.

The corporations finance the candidates for office; they put their hand-picked people into government regulatory agencies; they maintain massive lobbies on the state and national level; and through the lobbies, and through their political representatives, they determine the legislative fate of the country, **and** they divide up our tax dollars through grants, subsidies, and contracts.

I do a litmus test when I travel across the country. I ask people three questions. One, do you believe in democracy? Yes! Two, do you believe in one person, one vote? Yes! Three, do you believe that your vote has the same influence in the decision-making of this

52

country as Exxon, General Motors, and ITT? No one has ever said yes.

THIS TEAM WINS EVERY YEAR

Andrews in **The Daily World**, reprinted by permission.

Government of, by, and for the people?

Now, there are those who shout back that their vote shouldn't have the same influence as Exxon, General Motors and ITT because they are big corporations. Well, then, I say, if you believe that, and I'm sure there are people who do, then have the guts to stand up for what you believe in. Demand that it be written into the Constitution: Four branches of government.

Judicial. Congressional. Presidential. And **Corporate**. Demand that the Constitution prescribe how many votes General Motors and Exxon are to get in relation to the individual, sovereign citizens of this country. Let's make the reality a law, if we really believe it should be.

Corporations defy the concept of government of, by, and for the people. There is no doubt about it. The public opinion polls have shown it. According to a recent Gallup poll, 68% of the American people now believe the country is run of, by, and for big business. Only 7% of the people believe that they have some access in the affairs of government.

That's what the Bicentennial is all about. Democracy or rule by the few.

I don't know how long any reasonable person can continue to deny the facts. Buying elections, bribing the highest officials of our country, selling wheat to the Russian government so that they can charge higher prices for bread to the American consumer, intensifying a fake energy crisis in order to amass windfall profits, polluting the environment, and producing products each year which kill and maim thousands of Americans. All of these acts are committed against the citizens of this country by America's giant corporations. All these acts constitute treason.

And now the corporations are going to bring us the Bicentennial of the American Revolution!

What's the matter with commercialization of the Bicentennial? What's the matter with public relations tie-ins? Is there anyone in this room who could condone General Motors or Coca Cola bottling company using passages from the Bible and taking quotes from Jesus, Matthew, and Mark and plastering them on their products; identifying the founders of Christianity with their sales campaigns; is there anyone who would condone that? There is **no** difference between that and these corporations today exploiting the sacred principles that began this democratic nation by plastering them on Kellogg's Corn Flakes boxes and Spirit of America Chevrolets. At a time when millions of Americans are asking themselves the question "What Does America Stand For?" your corporations are so plasticizing the fundamental principles that we cherish as a people, as to make those principles absolutely meaningless for millions of people, who need desperately to renew their strength and patriotism in this country.

I don't believe that the giant corporations are fit to celebrate the Bicentennial of the Revolution. I believe that they are Tories in every sense of the word. A Tory, by the way, is an old Irish word. It means "thief," in case you are interested. So, I suggest that America's giant corporations be honest, that they identify with their true sentiments and interests, that they show their true colors and flag, royal purple, and that they conduct a Bicentennial fitting and proper for the place that they assume in American Society. I have taken the liberty of drafting up a new Declaration of Independence for Corporations. I hope that some energetic young public relations people will see some value in it.

We hold these truths to be self evident, that all business corporations are created equal. That they are endowed by their creator with certain unalienable rights. That among these are price-fixing, fraudulent advertising, and the pursuit of profit. That to secure these rights governments are bought by corporations deriving their just power from the consent of the stockholders. That whenever any form of government becomes destructive of these ends it is the right of the corporations to alter or abolish it and to finance new government, laying its foundation on such principles and organizing its power in such form as to them shall seem most likely to effect their safety and their profits.

RICH PREY ON POOR

Experience declares that man is the only animal which devours his own kind, for I can apply no milder term...to the general prey of the rich on the poor.

Thomas Jefferson, 1787

I believe the corporations are spitting on the American flag! I believe that they are undermining the democratic process! I believe that they have destroyed the principle of self-reliance and fostered the idea of

55

government handouts and a free ride mentality through subsidies and special favors! I believe they undermine the principle of personal responsibility and account- ability by engaging in wholesale crimes under the protection of that corporate charter! I believe they have robbed us, the American people, of the property of this country!

The American monopoly corporations have issued a death sentence against the individual human spirit, and that is what this experiment in nationhood started out to be.

Every day these giant bureaucratic prisons are draining every one of us in this country of that special energy that was to be our trademark and our destiny as a people. We all used to believe that we were each ''the captains of our fate and masters of our soul.'' Now, as I travel across the country, I see millions of footsoldiers in the giant corporate armies.

There is only one way to celebrate the Bicentennial of a revolution for democracy, for individual sover- eignty, and for a sense of shared community — and that is a new grassroots revolutionary movement to abolish these giant corporate tyrants which are destroying the fabric and fiber of this country. It is time to restore a sense of economic democracy here in America.

DISTINGUISHING FACT FROM OPINION

This discussion exercise is designed to promote experimentation with one's ability to distinguish between fact and opinion. It is a fact, for example, that the United States was militarily involved in the Vietnam War. But to say this involvement served the interests of world peace is an opinion or conclusion. Future historians will agree that American soldiers fought in Vietnam, but their interpretations about the causes and consequences of the war will probably vary greatly.

Some of the following statements are taken from readings in this chapter and some have other origins. Consider each statement carefully. Mark (**O**) for any statement you feel is an opinion or interpretation of the facts. Mark (**F**) for any statement you believe is fact. Then discuss and compare your judgments with those of other class members.

O = OPINION
F = FACT

_____1. Despite claims of "progressive taxation" the rich and super-rich have consistently provided themselves with legal gimmicks and loopholes to protect their huge fortunes.

_____2. In 1964, the Atlantic Oil Company paid no taxes on its earnings of $410 million.

_____ 3. The U.S. is one of the richest nations in the world.

_____ 4. To attack capitalism is not anti-American for the simple reason that most Americans are not capitalists.

_____ 5. The fact that, in a trillion dollar economy, we still have over thirty million Americans living in poverty is striking proof that our economy is owned by and for a very small elite.

_____ 6. Capitalism is the opposite of democracy since it is an economic system not owned by the people and run for the people, but a system owned and run by the rich.

_____ 7. Capitalism has provided people with the economic freedom to excel and create to their fullest potential.

_____ 8. Socialism would destroy economic freedom in America.

_____ 9. Americans have a high standard of living.

_____ 10. Our high standard of living is due mainly to our system of capitalism where people are free to pursue their creative talents and initiative.

_____ 11. Fears of economic concentration are unfounded and reflect a bias toward government intervention into the activities of business.

_____ 12. Today 200 giant corporations control two-thirds of the manufacturing assets of the United States of America.

_____ 13. With America's money, brains and social energy concentrated on the military, many medical and other social services have been allowed to become second rate.

_____ 14. The U.S. must continue to maintain a strong military to ensure our freedom and security.

THE FALLACIES
OF 'TRUST BUSTING'

M. Stanton Evans

M. Stanton Evans is an editor and author. He regularly contributes to conservative journals of social and political opinion. He writes frequently in **Human Events** and **American Opinion**, the latter a publication of the John Birch Society. He is also the Chairman of the American Conservative Union.

As you read consider the following questions:

1. Why does the author think ''trust busting'' is unnecessary?
2. What evidence does he cite to support his views?
3. How does the author describe the Goldberg study?

M. Stanton Evans, ''The Fallacies of 'Trust Busting,' '' **Human Events**, November 10, 1973, p. 12. Reprinted with permission.

As if things weren't tough enough for American business, the federal government and various states have launched themselves of late into another siege of "trust-busting."

The list of firms being dragged into court and before the regulator bodies these days is an impressive one: IBM, ITT, Ling-Timco-Vought, Xerox, Ford, GM, Goodyear, Firestone, the major oil companies, big steel, the cereal manufacturers, and so on. The general complaint is that these firms, by virtue of pricing policies, package selling and other practices, are somehow engaged in monopolistic activity.

Given the prevailing climate of opinion and the state of American legal theory, it is possible many of these alleged culprits will be found guilty and suffer economic deprivation as a result. Sen. Philip Hart (D.-Mich.), meanwhile, has even stronger medicine brewing: A "deconcentration" bill which would force divestiture in concentrated industries — defined as those in which four or fewer firms control 50 per cent of the market.

Fears about such matters have been heightened in recent years by steady publicity on the growth of conglomerates, and the supposed danger these present to the competitive market. The reigning faith in anti-trust circles is that mergers are bad, that unfettered industry will gravitate to a few highly concentrated firms, and that these firms will then be able to administer prices and gouge the public through collusion.

Such notions are not only entertained by Sen. Hart but have also been endorsed by former Atty. Gen. John Mitchell as the official creed of the Nixon Justice Department. Needless to remark, they are widely taught by academic economists and accepted as unquestioned fact on American campuses. So the idea that "concentration" is a natural blight of capitalism which government should work to prevent is almost universal doctrine.

Data to back this view, however, are slight to nonexistent. Empirical studies indicate there is not a natural tendency toward greater concentration, that where concentration does exist it is probably beneficial, and that conglomerate mergers do not in fact diminish

competition. These studies suggest that the only true monopolies in America are created by government — not the straw-men government seeks to combat.

Much of our thinking on this matter has consciously or unconsciously followed the dictum of Marx, who declared that "one capitalist kills many" and conjured up visions of small businesses being devoured by larger in a lurid spectacle of exploitation. Perhaps the most famous American formulation of the idea is that of Gardiner Means and Adolph Berle, who predicted back in the 1930s that according to then-prevailing trends, "seventy per cent of all corporate activity would be carried on by 200 corporations by 1950."

Nineteen-fifty came and went, however, with nothing of the sort occurring. Morris Adelman of MIT reviewed the evidence at that time and found, according to the rather variable criteria used to measure such things, that the general trend in our economy has been toward less economic concentration, not more. As he put it in a celebrated article in the **Review of Economics and Statistics:**

"...around 1901 nearly one-third of the value added by manufacture was produced in industries where the concentration ratio was 50 or more. Since then, there has been both further concentration and de-concentration. But the net result was that by 1947, only about one-fourth of value added was so produced.... The odds are better than even that there has actually been some decline in concentration."

Meticulous studies on this issue have been conducted by Warren Nutter, Edward Mason and numerous others, and the long-term data fail to bear out the concentration scare. Thus according to Nutter, some 32 per cent of manufacturing income at the turn of the century accrued to industries in which four firms accounted for half or more of the total production. By 1937, rather than increasing, this percentage had gone down to 28 per cent.

Mason adduces the corollary fact that in 1931 the 139 largest corporations accounted for some 49 per cent of the consolidated assets in the country. By 1949, the 139 largest accounted for 45 per cent. The wave of mergers up through the 1960s has to some extent reversed the trend, but as noted by Lawrence Goldberg in the **Journal of Law and Economics** the share of assets controlled by the 100 largest firms rose only from 45 to 47 per cent in the decade 1957-67.

As Prof. D.T. Armentano observes in his valuable study, **The Myths of Anti-Trust** (Arlington House; $11.95): "Even if concentration were a completely adequate and reliable measure of competition, there is surprisingly little empirical evidence that there has been any tendency for average market concentration to increase over time, and therefore for competition to decline.

"Studies of industrial concentration in the period 1901-1947, and some through 1968, have failed to reveal any significant or predictable upward trend...the popular and essentially Marxian hypothesis concerning an inevitable increase in industrial concentration has not been substantiated."

The kicker to all this is that, even where concentration exists, there is no convincing evidence that it is **per se** monopolistic. Prof. Harold Demsetz of UCLA has tackled this theory in his recent essay, **The Marxist Concentration Doctrine** (American Enterprise Institute-Hoover). He shows that studies purporting to demonstrate sustained higher rates of return in concentrated industries (supposed proof of monopoly) are based on thoroughly subjective evaluations of the data. He notes that a high return in any event may simply be evidence of greater efficiency, not "monopoly."

In like vein Prof. Yale Brozen rechecked the industries cited in such studies and found a constant regression toward the mean — that is, most high-profit industries had lower profits on re-checking, while most low-profit industries experienced an improvement in their rate of return. Whereas the study usually cited by concentration theorists showed a 4.4 per cent difference between the high and low concentration industries, in Brozen's update this difference was only 1.1 per cent.

Finally, Goldberg's study of the conglomerate questions suggests there is no empirical backing for the idea that mergers are hostile to competition.

Goldberg collected data on 44 conglomerate mergers

62

in which the growth of the acquired companies before and after merger could be measured. He found that "companies acquired in conglomerate mergers do not grow significantly faster than other companies. Acquisitions by larger companies are not more likely to accelerate the growth of acquired companies."

Where does all this leave prevailing theories on concentration and monopoly? The answer appears to be that such theories, like so much else that passes for wisdom in American public policy, are based on a deep-seated prejudice against the interplay of market forces and a bias toward government intervention. The available data suggest that the measure of monopoly is barrier to entry, not concentration — and barriers to entry are the work of government itself.

WHO NEEDS
A WAR ECONOMY?

Seymour Melman

Seymour Melman is pro-
fessor of industrial en-
gineering at Columbia
University. He is the
author of **Pentagon Cap-
Italism** and **The Permanent War Economy:
American Capitalism In
Decline**.

Think of the following questions while you read:

1. Who does the author say needs a war economy?
2. What does he claim have been the economic consequences of a war economy?
3. How do you interpret the cartoons in this reading?

Seymour Melman, "Who Needs A War Economy?" **The Nation**,
November 20, 1972, pp. 487, 488. Reprinted with permission.

"It's a helluva thing to say, but our economy needs a war. Defense spending should be increased to make more jobs for people."

Those are the words of a utility worker in Fredericksburg, W. Va., reported by the veteran opinion analyst Samuel Lubell in the August 14th |**Washington Star.** One of the things that Lubell discovered on a multi-state tour was that, "In every community sample the argument rages: do we need a war?"

During the last quarter century in the United States, an unspoken consensus has developed across political and ideological lines and across class lines. It is that a war economy encourages high employment and is in general good for prosperity. From being "good for" it is only a short step to "essential for."

For twenty-five years most of the nation's research and development talent, 80 per cent of federal research money, and the top technological institutes of the nation have been devoted to the military arts. Despite this effort — indeed, perhaps because of it — we have reached real limits of military power. It's no use having more or "better" nuclear weapons, since people can be destroyed only once. And the war in Vietnam is a bitter lesson on the limits of even the most powerful conventional armed forces.

At the same time, because talent, money and social energy are concentrated on the military, the civilian technology at the base of the American economy has been depleted. That is the main fact underlying the growing inability of many U.S. industries to compete in the world market and even the domestic market. Inability to serve an evident market is the hallmark of industrial depletion — economic and technological.

If these processes continue, economic and other deterioration of the U.S. economy and society can become irreversible. That irreversibility is reached when three conditions obtain: where there is no understanding of the causes of the problem; when there is available no theory of how to reconstruct the economy; and when there is available no corps of people who are technically competent to design and perform the industrial and other reconstruction.

'WHAT A FANTASTIC, NEW WEAPON —
EVEN BEFORE GOING INTO PRODUCTION,
IT'S DESTROYED OUR BUDGET'

Englehardt in the **St. Louis Post-Dispatch**

Who needs a war economy today? It is needed by the men in the White House and the Pentagon who are the top managers of the military-industrial empire. And it is needed by the employees — from highest to lowest — of the nonconvertible institutions of military economy. Nonconvertibility can be an inherent characteristic of some firms and institutions; it can also be created where it is not necessarily inherent. Thus, the obstinacy with which the most recent federal administrations have prevented planning for conversion from military to civilian economy has been a major contribution to nonconvertibility, thereby rendering a population hostage to a military economy.

SIZE OF MILITARY SECTOR

Some idea of the size of this military sector can be gained from the following statistics, cited in his book:

• By 1974, the real annual Pentagon budget, which includes payments for past, current, and future military operations, amounted to $123 billion, or 62 percent of the total "federal funds" budget of the government. This is more than 10 percent of the U.S. gross national product (GNP), and a sum greater than the GNP of all but a handful of countries.

• In 1971, the military accounted for 73 percent of the $97 billion of all federal purchases.

• By 1970 the value of military installations and material amounted to 38 percent of the total money value of all the assets of industry in the United States — $214 billion out of a total of $554 billion for all manufacturing corporations.

Dick Fidler, "The Cost of America's Permanent War Economy" (A book review of **The Permament War Economy** by Seymour Melman in **The Militant**), June 13, 1975, p. 20.

A war economy is one in which preparing for war or waging war is the dominant activity. What does "dominant" mean? In an industrial-capitalist economy, to dominate means first, to have priority control over capital. In 1939, for every dollar of corporate after-tax profit, military spending was $ .21. By 1971, for every dollar of corporate after-tax profit, the budget of the Department of Defense was $1.41. That means that by 1971 the Pentagon had superseded private firms in control over capital. Second, dominating industrial-capitalist economy means controlling industrial technology. For twenty-five years the military agencies of the federal government have dominated U.S. research and development: of $200 billion of federal money spent for R&D since World War II, 80 per cent was applied to defense, space and the Atomic Energy Commission. Third, the military agencies, by virtue of their control over research, have strongly influenced the curricula for training the people who carry in their minds the possibility of creating new technology. Together with technical research, they are the core production of an industrial society.

On functional economic grounds one can and must differentiate between military and nonmilitary work and production. Nonmilitary activity contributes to the level of living or to capability for further production of all kinds. Military activity does not contribute economically either to the level of living or to further production.

What have been the economic consequences of a war economy sustained over a quarter century? I shall identify twenty such consequences for American society:

(1) The federal government has become the chief controller of the economy by controlling capital and the largest number of employees.

(2) Twenty thousand firms, serving the military and directed by the Pentagon have been able to maximize cost, and thus also government subsidy, as a way to maintain or enlarge the decision power of management.

(3) One-half to two-thirds of the science and engineering research brains of the nation have been concentrated on military and related technology.

(4) Engineering and technical schools have been oriented to produce technology relevant to the military. Thus, while electronics for aerospace has been elaborately developed, power engineering has been neglected.

(5) The United States has developed an extraordinarily high ratio of military expenditure to gross domestic fixed investment. During 1967-69 the U.S. ratio was 52.8 per cent; in West Germany it was 14 per cent; in Japan, 2.3.

(6) U.S. civilian industry has become increasingly hardpressed to offset the difference between American and foreign wage rates. For a century this country was able to compensage for cheaper foreign labor by sustaining a high enough level of productivity per worker so that products were competitive on the home market. That competence is being eroded in many U.S. industries.

(7) As a further consequence of growing inability to compete, key U.S. industries have been losing their positions in the world market as well. For example, the American machine-tool industry was first in the world until a few years ago; it is now in third place and is also losing the technological edge that is based on innovation in research and design.

(8) The U.S. economy has developed and sustained an imbalance of trade and an imbalance of payments unfavorable to the United States.

(9) The country has been losing its gold reserves and its ability to redeem dollars held abroad in gold or other hard currency; as a result, the financial, and allied political, competence of the U.S. Government has declined.

(10) U.S. factories have been moving abroad in search of superior opportunities for investment and growth. This has cost the United States at least 1 million jobs.

(11) The flight of capital from the United States is unprecedented in the economic history of any country. In 1961 the United States had $31 billion in directed investments abroad. By 1971 an additional $47 billion of

capital had left the country. This outflow is an unspoken opinion of the viability of American economy and society — cast mainly by American-based multinational corporations.

(12) A rapid price inflation is eroding earnings and savings of every sort.

(13) Technical and economic depletion besets the industries that serve the domestic market. For example, the present housing industry cannot offer a product that is salable or rentable to the less affluent half of the population. Where are the social energies, the money and the brains that would be needed for any serious effort to reconstruct this important industry? Secretary Romney recently complained to the Congress that the entire budget for his Department of Housing and Urban Development was not even half as great as the budget assigned to the Department of Defense for research and development alone.

(14) The services provided for the domestic population are deteriorating. With money, brains and social energy concentrated on the military, many medical services have been allowed to become second rate. Thus the wealthiest country in the world ranks fourteenth among nations in infant mortality rates and eighth in the ratio of doctors to population. Last year the United States, alone among large countries, showed a decline in the life expectancy of adult males. The American College of Surgeons and recently the National Academy of Science have called attention to the calamitous condition of emergency medical care in the United States.

(15) The war economy has been using up the capital fund that would be needed for economic development and reconstruction in the United States. Thus our military expenditures since 1945 amount to $1,300 billion, a sum exceeding the value of all residential and all commercial structures on the surface of the United States. What has been expended is equivalent to the capital that would be required literally to reconstruct most of the country. Instead, we have bought armed forces and bases for a program of Vietnam-type wars, and the ability to annihilate every Soviet city twenty-seven times over.

(**16**) The war economy has used up the capital funds needed to sponsor economic development abroad. One consequence is a growing gap between levels of living and of industrial development generally in the have and have-not nations of the world.

(**17**) The U.S. Government has become the world's largest merchant of arms.

BOTTOMLESS PIT

Andrews in **The Daily World**, reprinted by permission.

(18) Ten per cent of the U.S. labor force has become directly dependent on the military economy for employment and income. This 10 per cent, concentrated by state, industry and occupation, has been made into a hostage for continuing the war economy. That is the result of successful prevention of all conversion planning by the federal government.

(19) The war economy is increasingly being used by the federal executive as an instrument for manipulating general economic activity.

(20) A given state's participation in the war economy is cited by members of Congress as an indicator of the services they have rendered to their communities.

Americans (but no other people) learned a spurious wisdom from the experience of World War II. Two ideas emerged: first, that the industrial capacity of the United States is so indefinitely large as to make possible virtually any combination of guns and butter; second, that military economy means jobs for all and a general economic prosperity. Obviously, the 1940-45 war economy put an end to the unemployment of the Great Depression.

Unnoticed by Americans, however, were the special qualities of the country's World War II experience. U.S. participation lasted only four years, during which the labor force was enlarged by the addition of women, old, young, black, Spanish-speaking Americans and by lengthened work week and work year. The job market has not shriveled, while the continuing war economy fans inflation. It was crucial that the United States never suffered the consequences of military operations on its soil. There was no destruction of U.S. capital facilities. The roads, the railroads, the steel mills, the housing — all lasted through four years without major replacement. Now they are becoming obsolete compared with standards in other industrialized states, and twenty-five years of cold war show that the United States is no exception to the rule that ''guns'' are a drain on ''butter.''

For all that, the ideologies justifying a war economy as economically beneficial are still with us. These ideologies have helped to sustain a twenty-five-year war economy, in the manner of a ''self-fulfilling prophecy.''

MORE DEFENSE SPENDING NEEDED

John L. McLucas

John L. McLucas is the Secretary of the Air Force of the United States. He made the following comments as part of a speech delivered before the Harvard Law School Forum in Cambridge, Massachusetts, on February 13, 1975.

Use the following questions to assist your reading:

1. What effect does the author say inflation has had on the defense budget?
2. Why does he claim that now is not the time to relax our military posture?
3. What is the message of the cartoon in this reading?

John L. McLucas, ''The Military Balance,'' **Vital Speeches**, April 1, 1975, pp. 358-60. Reprinted with permission.

About this time every year, the federal budget proposed by the President is being given initial scrutiny by the Congress and is prominent in newspapers and other media. For a number of years there also have been calls to cut defense spending, and this year is no exception. Moreover, in the last few years some Americans have asked why we can't significantly reduce our defense bill in an era of detente.

It seems to me that there are two basic parts to the answer — inflation and military balance. I'd like to take a little time to talk about each of these points with you this evening.

Impact of Inflation

In discussing inflation, I'm sure that I don't have to convince anyone here that it has had a serious impact on all of us. However, I'm afraid that many people do not realize just how serious has been its effect on national defense.

Since 1968 the purchasing power of the Department of Defense budget has declined some 40 percent, even though the funding level in then-year dollars has remained more or less level. In the fiscal year 1975 budget alone, it looks like we have already lost $6 billion to inflation.

If we take a longer perspective, the effect is even more dramatic. For example, the 1953 budget, which represented a peak year in the 50s, was close to $50 billion. In constant 1975 dollars that figure would be about $120 billion.

My point is that whatever the dollar figures for any year may be, it is necessary to consider what they can be converted to in terms of the real defense resources needed to do the job.

One example you are probably familiar with is the cost of fuel. The Air Force has made a great effort to conserve energy. As a result, we expect that consumption of fuel this year will be 27 percent less than it was in 1973. Yet because of the increased price of oil, our cost will be more than twice as much as in 1973. We have learned to live with that much less fuel, but not with double and triple costs.

Incidentally, trying to predict the rate of inflation is extremely difficult, and as a result we sometimes get into difficulty in our cost estimates. From time to time you have heard of cost increases in particular defense programs; but especially in recent years, a great deal of the increase often can be attributed to higher inflation rates. In the B-1 strategic bomber program that is so necessary to our defense, we anticipated in our 1970 estimate of total program cost that about one-eighth would be due to inflation. Today we estimate that inflation will amount to almost one half of the toal cost. A 1 percent change in the average inflation rate compounded over the remaining decade of B-1 acquisition produces about a $1 billion change in the total cost. To put it another way, if we discount inflation the current estimate for the cost of a B-1 is 34.3 million 1970 dollars, an increase of less than 12 percent since the program began.

Thus I think it is very clear that inflation is one major reason why we haven't been able to lower the apparent defense budget. In fact, so serious has been its impact that the more appropriate question probably should be, How have we managed to keep from substantially increasing the budget? Indeed, the 40 percent cut in purchasing power since 1968 has not been matched by similar cuts in responsibilities. The nation still expects adequate military security. It also hopes for further progress in detente. Both of these goals depend upon maintaining a worldwide military balance. This is not to say that military power alone is sufficient, but it is the indispensable foundation.

The Military Balance

Apparently for some people, detente and strength are incompatible. Perhaps this view is based on the idea that strength produces tension and conflict. While I would argue that lack of adequate strength can produce just as much, if not more, tension and conflict, I think the real point to be remembered is that detente is a mixture of cooperation and competition, and a very delicate one at that. We need to be acutely aware of detente's limitations as well as its advantages. In 1975, it is not yet based on the complete altruism of man, but rather upon mutual interests, most particularly, avoiding the catastrophe of nuclear war. Political, military, and economic developments of the past few years have brought us to this relationship of detente, and we are hopeful for the future, but now is not the time to relax our military posture. If we are no longer in a cold war, we are not yet in a stable peace.

Certainly, detente has not stopped the Soviet Union from continuing to increase its military power. The CIA estimates that Soviet defense expenditures became larger than ours in fiscal 1971, which was shortly after we began to withdraw from Southeast Asia. It is difficult, of course, to make precise calculations of dollar costs of Soviet programs; nevertheless, it is clear that their defense budget is substantially more than ours, probably about 20 percent greater in 1974. This trend of greater Soviet defense expenditures compared to those of the United States has very serious implications....

Reprinted with permission of the **Manchester, New Hampshire Union Leader**.

Why the U.S.?

Yet for some, there is still the question of why it should be the United States that carries this broad responsibility. In short, because no other country can — and someone must! Only the United States has the strength to match the power of the Soviet Union. Only we can insure the military balance that is capable of deterring the other superpower.

Let me illustrate why we must provide the balance. In the strategic forces area, the United States is the only nation that can maintain an assured destruction capability against the Soviet Union. That is, only we can maintain the strategic forces to convince a Soviet planner contemplating a first strike that our surviving forces would still be sufficient to inflict unacceptable damage upon the Soviet Union. Morever, only the U.S. can provide credible "nuclear umbrellas" to our allies. Therefore, it is the United States that must deter nuclear war.

History supports the old dictum that war results

from a perceived imbalance of military power, not a balance. Last August, shortly after he took office, President Ford pledged "continuity in the loyal collaboration" with our allies. We remain a leader of a free association of nations. While we neither are, nor aspire to be, the policeman of the world, we certainly remain the principal contributor to an active system of collective security.

Conclusion.

In summary, the defense budget, like yours, is a victim of inflation. But more importantly, its size also reflects the will of the American people that it should take into account the realities of growing Soviet military power and the consequent international responsibilities of the United States.

Of course, we as a people may elect to withdraw from that responsibility, but before we do, we should realize the consequences. As Secretary of Defense Schlesinger pointed out last month in New York, "Unless we are prepared to defend portions of the world lying outside of North America, we shall soon find ourselves with nothing else but North America to defend." He then emphasized that "under those circumstances ...the portion of national effort going to defense would increase dramatically rather than diminish." That cannot be a happy prospect for anyone, whether his concern be domestic social progress, national security, or personal liberty. Today, it is a situation that we can still decide to avoid.

SOCIAL CHANGE AND PRIORITIES

SOCIAL CHANGE AND PRIORITIES

In an effort to deal with economic and social problems and to promote a sense of justice, our nation must examine its values and priorities. Do we need social change, or should things remain essentially the same? Should we do some things the way people did in the past or radically alter some institutions around new ideas? If change is needed, how quickly should it come? How might social change hurt some people, and should the government compensate them?

The following exercise will explore your attitude toward social change and priorities. Sometimes change brings progress, other times pain and suffering; and frequently both progress and human suffering are by-products of social, political, scientific, and techno-logical change. Change can occur slowly or it can come suddenly and quickly (revolutionary change).

Consider each of the following items and statements carefully. Then, at your desk or in small groups of four to six, pick 12 items or priorities that you feel most need action or consideration by our political leaders and institutions. Then discuss and compare your decisions with those of other class members.

_____1. A more equal distribution of the wealth

_____2. A better system of national defense

_____3. A better quality of life through severe restrictions on industries that would help protect our national environment and limited natural resources against pollution and abuse

_____4. Relaxation of environmental restrictions so industries will have more incentives to invest in new projects that will stimulate the economy and create jobs

_____5. A more effective system of criminal justice (courts, police, prisons, etc.)

_____6. An improved system of education

_____7. More emphasis on space exploration

_____8. An end to discrimination

_____9. More resources directed toward defending others and ourselves against Communist advances

_____10. An end to poverty (slums, hunger, malnutrition, and etc.)

_____11. Encouragement of competitive values to stimulate economic activity and improved performance in all fields

_____12. Security for elderly people, and the mentally and physically handicapped

_____13. Promotion of continued industrial growth and consumption of consumer goods to stimulate the economy

_____14. Development of solar, geothermal, wind, and other forms of non-polluting energy sources

_____15. Less Federal Government restrictions on business and industrial activities

_____16. Better health care at a cost everyone can afford

_____17. Less spending by the Federal Government on welfare and other social programs

_____18. Laws preventing or discouraging the production of ''gas-guzzling'' and polluting cars

_____19. Reduced federal taxes and a balanced budget

_____20. Laws and restrictions against producing goods that are designed to wear out quickly

_____21. More care taken about too much tampering and interference with the CIA, FBI, and other military and criminal investigative agencies that protect our internal security and fight crime

_____22. The development of mass transit

_____23. Less control by the Federal Government over the state governments so each state can work out its own creative solutions to problems

_____24. Encouragement of cooperative values to make our society a less materialistic, greedy and threatening place in which to live

_____25. Reduced state taxes and balanced state budgets

_____26. More curbs on the CIA, FBI, and other military and criminal investigating agencies that have illegally spied on millions of Americans for political reasons

3 CHAPTER

SOCIAL
JUSTICE

THE CASE FOR THE EQUAL RIGHTS AMENDENT

Marguerite Rawalt

Marguerite Rawalt is the Past National President of the National Association of Women Lawyers, and the National Federation of Business and Professional Women's Clubs. She is now the National Chairwoman for the Equal Rights Amendment Ratification of the Women's Equity Action League.

As you read try to answer the following questions:

1. Why does the author say that the woman who works in the home is most in need of the Equal Rights Amendment?
2. How does she describe state laws calling for a husband to support his family?
3. Why does she claim that the draft is no excuse for opposing the Equal Rights Amendment?
4. Can you relate the cartoon in this reading to the author's ideas?

Reprinted from speeches by Marguerite Rawalt on the Equal Rights Amendment.

The HOMEMAKER, the woman who works in the home without salary, more than other classes of women, is in need of the Equal Rights Amendment. She is the "forgotten woman" under the Constitution and state laws of today. Her "career" would gain recognition under the ERA.

The English common law is the basis of our Constitution and of the statutes in 42 states. Under its principles, when a woman marries she loses her separate legal identity on the theory that husband and wife are one, and the husband is the one. Upon her marriage, the wife loses her name, her individual credit rating if she had one, independent control over her property and its earnings, and her legal domicile.

Marital property rights under the Common Law

The years of labor of the wife in the home, the bearing of children, acting as baby sitter, child counselor and guide, housekeeper, household financial manager, are all without salary or wages. As a chattel of her husband she owes him her services and labor under common law principles. There is one outstanding exception. When a husband brings a common law action for loss of consortium (damages for loss of wife's affection, companionship, society and sexual relations) the courts have no difficulty in placing money values upon her services in order to allow him recovery against the third party liable for having caused physical injury to his wife (e.g. auto-train accident). Thus, by being rendered permanently injured, or crippled for life, the wife can generate legal recognition of a value for her services, with payment therefore to the husband! In most jurisdictions no reciprocal recovery is allowable to a wife whose husband is permanently injured.

Since no money value is placed upon the wife's labors in the home, she is not counted as making any investment or contribution to the acquisition of the marital property, be it the home residence or a business which her husband may operate. The marital property is that of her husband. In the case of dissolution of the marriage by divorce, she can only petition the court for a share of her **husband's property**. Her claims to a share of property are decided by the court, more often than not upon a compromise agreement reached

Scott Long in **The Minneapolis Tribune**.

between opposing attorneys. It is to the husband's advantage to label as much as possible as "alimony" which is tax deductible by him and taxable to her, rather than as maintenance or support, which is not deductible. And should her father leave her an inheritance, her husband becomes entitled to share the income and often to control and manage her separate property.

In the eight community property states, founded upon the French and Spanish Codes, husband and wife have equal ownership; however, the husband generally has independent management and control of the whole. In other countries, marriage has been recognized as an economic partnership between equals. Such a marital partnership and ownership and division of property upon divorce is recognized in the proposed Uniform Marriage and Divorce Act which has been approved by the American Bar Association for adoption by the states. Under its provisions the Court would be required to place a money value on the years of work by the wife in the home.

The Equal Rights Amendment would support a recognition of partnership rights and ownership in marital property based upon the valuation of the wife's contribution to its acquisition. It would be in harmony with the proposed Uniform Act and with laws of many other nations.

Husband's duty of support

State laws calling for a husband to support his family go no further than a duty to provide what the law calls "necessaries." And the law makes the husband the sole judge of what constitutes "necessaries" of food and shelter. If he never allowed her to own more than one pair of shoes, or to have an air conditioner, or to have a kitchen sink or a food freezer (as Mrs. McGuire) she has no legal redress. He can stop her credit for groceries and clothing at any time.

So long as she lives under his roof, the wife has no right to go to court for an increase in support allowance from her husband. This is a cardinal principle of common law upon which statutes in 42 states are premised. She must sue to break up the marriage if she wishes to challenge her support allowance.

The leading case, found in law school textbooks, declares the principle that "to maintain an action such as the one at bar, the parties must be separated or living apart from each other...." In that case, the wife of a well-to-do farmer for 34 years sued for support allowance. The husband forbade her any charge accounts, refused to provide any modern running water or electric appliances in the home, or to purchase a replacement for a 24-year-old automobile. The court held that he was providing the "necessaries of life."

"A woman's best insurance of proper support is to marry a good man." And because most husbands are good men, homemaker wives never have occasion to learn of the legal inequities which could beset a less fortunate one. It is not believed that decent men support their wives and families only because of a legal compulsion. Wives, like husbands, already have a legal duty of support in many states where the husband is incapacitated — a duty to provide "necessaries."

The ERA would recognize an economic partnership between spouses, as the law is now rapidly approaching. It would give the wife legal status to seek redress in courts. It would give new dignity to the important roles of mother and housewife. The homemaker needs the Equal Rights Amendment.

The Equal Rights Amendment and the DRAFT

The fact that women may become subject to the draft when the Equal Rights Amendment is adopted is no acceptable alibi for opposing ratification by the members of State legislatures. Nor should it be tolerated as a threat to intimidate women in their efforts to gain recognition of individual legal rights inherent in the very principles of a democratic society. Let us look at the facts of the draft.

1. Under the Selective Service law only those aged 18 to 26 are subject to the draft. And, only those classified I-A are called, by lottery system. The draft has never proceeded beyond Class I-A to call in any deferred class.

EQUAL PAY

DISTORTION: "ERA won't give women anything they don't already have or have a way of getting. For example: Women can get equal pay through the 1964 Civil Rights Act and the 1972 Equal Employment Opportunity Act."

FACT: These acts fail to cover women in small companies which have no federal contracts and which do not deal in interstate commerce. Many people who are aware of a constitutional amendment are unaware of their protection under less significant legislation. Those who do know, try one by one to get enforcement in specific cases. This is a slow and tedious process. This piecemeal litigation could go on indefinitely, without providing basic constitutional protection for all.

Glenn E. Watts, "The Equal Rights Amendment," Communications Workers of America Pamphlet.

2. There is no substance to the charge that mothers would be dragged from their children to serve on the front lines in combat duty. No one will be drafted so long as he has a deferment. Under the law, young men are deferred to Class III-A because of hardship on dependents, and dependents may be wife, child, parent, or even grandparents. Would young women be treated more restrictively? Deferments are fixed by regulations approved by the President.

3. The 1971 draft call, officially reported, reveals that less than 25% of all men of draft age were ever subjected to the draft in the first place, because of rejections.

Only 5% of the eligible males in the country were actually inducted into the services in that year.

Less than 1% of eligible males in the whole country were ever assigned to combat units, and only a fraction of those to the front lines. These figures cannot be disputed. (Cong. Rec. 3/21/72, pp. S.4389-4391). Combat duty would thus, at most, apply to an extremely small percentage of females if at all.

THE CASE AGAINST THE EQUAL RIGHTS AMENDENT

Phyllis Schlafly

Phyllis Schlafly is a leading opponent of the Equal Rights Amendment. She has testified against the Amendment before Congressional Committees and at numerous state legislative hearings. She has appeared on many radio and television programs and has written articles for **Human Events, The Independent American, New Guard** and other conservative publications.

The following questions should help you examine the reading:

1. Why does the author say ERA will do nothing for women in the field of employment?
2. How does she say ERA will effect women in relation to the draft?
3. What effect does she say ERA will have on women in the area of labor legislation?
4. How do you interpret the cartoons in this reading?

Phyllis Schlafly, ''Let's Stop ERA,'' **New Guard**, September, 1973, pp. 4-6. Reprinted with permission.

ERA and Employment

Many people have naively supported the Equal Rights Amendment because they felt that it would guarantee equal pay for equal work, and improve the status of women in regard to employment. When I debated Congresswoman Martha Griffiths on the Lou Gordon television show, I said that ERA will do absolutely nothing for women in the field of employment. Mrs. Griffiths replied, ''I never said it would.''

I have testified at 12 state legislative hearings, and in not a single one has a pro-ERA lawyer stated that ERA will do anything whatsoever for women in the field of employment. They know that, in the first place, ERA applied only to Federal and state laws, and not to private employment at all; and secondly, the Equal Employment Opportunity Act of 1972 already guarantees women everything in the field of employment which can be done by legislation.

This law is very specific in regard to hiring, pay and promotions. If any woman thinks she has been discriminated against, she can file her claim with the government and the government will pay all the costs. When AT&T was recently forced to pay $38 million by the Equal Employment Opportunity Commission, this proved that the legislative machinery is fully adequate; the only thing remaining is enforcement.

At the various state legislative hearings around the country, ERA proponenets have failed to make a case that a constitutional amendment is needed or would provide any constructive benefits to women. They are still crying around about obsolete discriminations against women which have not existed in the memory of most of us alive today. They are still weeping about women not having the right to vote, women not being able to serve on juries, women not being able to attend college or become lawyers, and other discriminations which disappeared decades ago.

At the ERA hearing in Virginia, the star witness was a 93-year-old woman who said she was an original suffragette and had been campaigning for women's rights since 1909. She concluded her testimony by saying that the proponents of the Equal Rights Amendment have the mentality of 50 years ago, and they are fighting a

battle that is long since won. She received a standing ovation.

Drafting Women?

The matter of the draft really reveals the hypocrisy of the ERA proponents. The Equal Rights Amendment will positively make women subject to the draft, and on an equal basis with men. This means running the same obstacle courses, carrying the same 40-50 pound packs, serving in combat and on warships, and all the other dangerous and unpleasant duties. ERA would not permit a system whereby the women would have all the easy desk jobs, with the men assigned to the unpleasant and fighting jobs. ERA would mandate equality across the board.

Most of the ERA proponents are, of course, safely past draft age, a fact which should be kept in mind when they talk so glibly about welcoming the drafting of women. Of the draft-age women who are whooping it up for ERA, most of them — when questioned personally about the draft — hesitate, and then reserve to themselves the right to be a conscientious objector or evade military service in some way.

The ERA proponents say that Congress already has the power to draft women. This is true — but Congress has used this power to exempt women, and that is the way we like it. The overwhelming majority of American men and women do **not** want women drafted, and they don't realize that making women subject to the draft is a precedent-shattering sleeper in ERA.

Anyone who really favors the drafting of women — and there are some — should work for it in the honest, above-board way, that is, by proposing an amendment to the Selective Service Act. Then the issue could be debated and our citizens would know the consequences. The ERA proponents are trying to put over this massive change in our social mores without the majority even realizing what is happening.

ERA proponents also argue that the draft has ended and we will have a volunteer military. It is a very naive person who looks into the future and says, "We are going to have no more wars and no more draft." We are very fortunate that ERA was not ratified 10 years ago, else there would have been thousands of additional tragedies in Vietnam.

The proponents talk about the "benefits" women will receive under the draft. Well, we must also include the "benefits" of being shipped thousands of miles away to fight a jungle war in Southeast Asia, and the "benefits" of being a prisoner of war, and the "benefits" of being missing in action. These are not the kind of "benefits" women want.

Barnett in the **New Guard**, reprinted by permission.

The Sledgehammer Approach

The Equal Rights Amendment is like trying to kill a fly with a sledgehammer. You probably won't kill the fly, but you surely will break up some furniture. For example, the laws of every one of our 50 states now make it the obligation of the husband to support his wife and family. This is based on the obvious fact that it is the women who have the babies and, therefore, it should be the men who provide the financial support.

The Equal Rights Amendment will invalidate these state laws in every one of the 50 states because no longer can we have any legislation which imposes an obligation on one sex which it does not impose equally on the other. Removing these state laws will take away from the wife her legal right to be a fulltime wife and mother, supported by her husband.

The result is confirmed by the pro-ERA lawyers who testify at the hearings. They admit that they do want to remove the full obligation of the husband and make the obligation for financial support of the family fall **equally** on the husband **and** the wife. Such a legalistic equality would impose a realistic double burden on the wife, because she is still the one who will have the babies.

Labor Legislation

A third area of concern is the matter of protective labor legislation. Women who work in industry are protected by many laws, provisions in union contracts, and company policies which guarantee their right to be treated like a woman. The Equal Rights Amendment will wipe these all out, and the proponents say this is what they want.

A woman can compete equally with a man in intellectual, professional, and academic occupations because women are just as smart as men. However, a woman can**not** compete equally with a man in manual labor or in physical work because she is **not** as strong. Anyone who doubts this truism should look at the Olympic Games. If the men and women competed with each other in the Olympics, the women would simply not win any gold, silver or bronze medals.

The fourth area is Social Security. When a working woman retires, she now receives a higher financial payment than a man who has worked the same number of years at the same salary. All preferential treatment for women would be wiped out by the Equal Rights Amendment.

Hayden Modification

During most of the time that the Equal Rights Amendment was in Congress, and during the time when many prominent people became committed to the

Equal Rights Amendment, it had attached to it another clause called the Hayden Modification which read, "The provisions of this Article shall not be construed to impair any rights, benefits or exemptions conferred by law upon persons of the female sex."

This clause was struck out under agitation from the women's liberationists. It shows very clearly that the effect of the Equal Rights Amendment would be precisely to deprive wives of the right to be supported by their husband, of the benefits that working women have under protective labor legislation and the Social Security, and of the exemption that draft-age girls have from the military.

There is another section of ERA called Section 2 which shifts to Congress the power to implement the Equal Rights Amendment by appropriate legislation. This is a grab for power at the federal level, pure and simple. It will remove from the state legislatures, the bodies closest to the will of the people, the authority to legislate in the entire field of women's rights, including criminal law, property rights or anything pertaining to domestic relations. All this will be transferred out of the hands of the state legislature and into the hands of Congress, the executive branch, and the federal courts.

Proponents' Tactics

Unable to answer the arguments about the rights women now possess which they will lose if ERA is ratified, the ERA proponents have shifted their tactics. Time and time again, instead of trying to make an affirmative case for ERA, the proponents resort to abusing their opponents. One of their favorite tactics is to accuse the opponents of being financed by a giant conspiracy made up of the Communist Party, the Ku Klux Klan, the AFL-CIO, the John Birch Society, and the Catholic and Mormon Churches. The ridiculousness of this charge is self-evident. One wag suggested that anyone who could get all those groups together ought to be nominated for the Nobel Peace Prize!

Another tactic is to argue that, since ERA passed Congress by very large majorities, it must deserve our support. In essence, this argument is, Big Brother in Washington, D.C. knows best.

The fact is that the story is now leaking out as to why some of the senators and congressmen voted for the Equal Rights Amendment a year ago. One prominent senator frankly admitted to his constituents that he voted for it only "to get those militant women off my back." Another well-known senator said he voted for it because of "sheer terror."

A third prominent senator said he knew it was a piece of bad legislation, but voted for it anyway. Congress' passage of ERA was a classic case of buckpassing to the state legislatures.

Having failed to demonstrate any legal rights which women will gain through ERA, the proponents have fallen back on the argument that it is "symbolic" and needed for " psychological" objectives. But the United States Constitution should not be turned into an instrument to provide a psychological cure for personal problems.

The first dozen states that ratified the ERA did so without hearings or debate. They just called it up and passed it because they thought women wanted it. Now, the legislators are having second thoughts. One-third of the states that ratified ERA in 1972 are considering motions to rescind. On March 15, 1973, the Nebraska Legislature rescinded its earlier ratification of the Equal Rights Amendment. When Alabama on June 12, 1973 voted 26 to 6 to reject ERA, it became the 20th state to reject the Equal Rights Amendment.

The ERA proponents have promised to continue the fight for six more years, but we hope the state legislators will not be stampeded into accepting an amendment which, like Prohibition, they will surely regret.

UNDERSTANDING STEREOTYPES

INSTRUCTIONS

A stereotype is an oversimplified or exaggerated description. It can apply to things or people and be favorable or unfavorable. Quite often stereotyped beliefs about racial, religious, and national groups are insulting and oversimplified. They are usually based on misinformation or lack of information.

"I KNOW WE'RE HOME FROM VIET NAM.. BUT NOW I GET THE FEELING WE'RE SURROUNDED BY THE REAL ENEMY."

Muhammed Speaks, April 13, 1973.

PART I

The cartoon above is an example of stereotyping. Examine the cartoon carefully and, with other class members, discuss why it is an example of stereotyping.

PART II

Read through the following list carefully. Mark (**S**) for any statement that is an example of stereotyping. Mark (**N**) for any statement that is not an example of stereotyping. Mark (**U**) if you are undecided about any statement. Then discuss and compare your decisions with other class members.

S = **Stereotype**
N = **Not a stereotype**
U = **Undecided**

_____1. Communists believe in violent social change and are opposed to democracy.

_____2. Many black people have made valuable social contributions.

_____3. Africa is a land of rain forests and jungles.

_____4. Americans are generally happier than the people who live in China.

_____5. People in Europe have basic needs that are similar to those of the people of Asia.

_____6. Women tend to be less aggressive and competitive than men.

_____7. The American government does not endorse racial separation.

_____8. Democratic countries are less warlike than Communist nations.

_____9. Black people are skilled at dancing, singing, and athletics.

_____10. Poor people tend to be careless and disorderly.

_____11. In many countries minority groups are discriminated against.

_____12. Intellectuals are generally not very practical people.

_____13. For most Jews money is the most important thing in life.

_____14. Communist nations are imperialistic and devious.

_____15. Men are better qualified than women for highly responsible and powerful political positions.

_____16. It takes skill and training to become an accountant.

_____17. Women are not suited for military service.

_____18. Foreign ideas can often be a threat to the American way of life.

_____19. Wealthy people seldom work hard.

_____20. Economic problems in America today are similar to American economic problems of earlier times.

HISTORIANS DENIGRATE INDIAN VIRTUES

Virgil J. Vogel

Virgil J. Vogel is Associate Professor of History at Mayfair College in Chicago. The following article is excerpted from an essay-review of historical books on the American Indian published by Integrated Education.

Consider the following questions while reading:

1. How does the author say historians have created and perpetuated false impressions of aboriginal Americans?
2. What four methods does he say they have used?
3. How do the cartoons in this reading support the author's ideas?
4. What specific contributions does he say the Indians have made?

Virgil J. Vogel, "The Indian In American History," Integrated Education Associates, 1968. Reprinted with permission.

Historians have used four principal methods to create or perpetuate false impressions of aboriginal Americans, namely: **obliteration**, **defamation**, **disembodiment**, and **disparagement**. Often the four methods overlap and interlace with one another. Their use does not necessarily flow from conscious malice. More probably, they result from confinement within the narrow limits of the discipline, unfamiliarity with the other social sciences, and the mindsets and assumptions imposed by the historian's own cultural background. The following remarks are based on an examination of more than a hundred books, mainly, but not entirely, designed for use as history texts. Space will permit citing only a few which typify the attitudes we seek to illustrate.

OBLITERATION

Perhaps the chief problem in the historical treatment of American Indians and other minorities is not the biased presentation, but the blackout....

During the nineteenth century the early extermination of the Indian was freely predicted, and even advocated. It is a persistent theme in commentaries of the period, of which Francis Parkman serves as a typical example:

"Their intractable, unchanging character leaves no alternative than their gradual extinction, or the abandonment of the western world to eternal barbarism; and of this and similar plans...it may alike be said that sentimental philanthropy will find it easier to cavil at than to amend them." [1]

Although these genocidal aims fell short of accomplishment, the historical obliteration of the Indian was more nearly successful. The treatment of the Jackson era is a revealing case study. One of the cruelest ordeals of the American Indian occurred during the administration of Andrew Jackson and his immediate successor, Martin Van Buren, when more than 125,000 of them were dragged from their homes and deported west of the Mississippi by military force. The "treaties" which preceded these expulsions (94 of them in Jackson's time) were masterpieces of intimidation, bribery, threats, misrepresentation, force, and fraud. Following these efforts to produce a fig-leaf of legality for the operation, Indians were hunted down like animals, bound as prisoners, and confined in stockades to await removal. The conditions of the deportation were so barbarous that about one third of the emigres died on the journey. [2] In the few cases where open resistance was encountered, as with Black Hawk's Sauks, the defiant Indians were massacred.... [3]

"AS YOU WELL KNOW, WE CONSISTENTLY FIGHT FOR INDIAN RIGHTS AND WE HONOR EVERY TREATY."

Andrews in **The Daily World**, reprinted by permission.

In **The Age of Jackson**, by Arthur M. Schlesinger, Jr.,[4] there is not one word about the "Trail of Death."[5]

To draw the curtain over unpleasant happenings in history is not less to be deplored than conscious falsification. The selectivity of the historian is revealing. If omitted events are of a sort which would dampen the impression the writer seeks to create, we are getting historical fiction, for only novelists can take such liberties. Silence cannot save us from the stain of our Indian policies....

DISEMBODIMENT

This school acknowledged the existence of the Indian, but only as a subhuman nomad, a part of the fauna belonging to the wilderness yet to be conquered; in short, a troublesome **obstacle** to be overcome. "We may guess," wrote the Puritan preacher Cotton Mather, "that probably the devil decoyed those miserable savages hither, in hopes that the gospel of the Lord Jesus Christ would never come here to destroy or disturb his **absolute empire** over them." [6] No moral restraint was required in dealing with them. As late as 1872, this attitude found voice in remarks of U.S. Indian Commissioner Francis Walker:

"With wild men, as with wild beasts, the question of whether in a given situation one shall fight, coax, or run, is a question merely of what is easiest and safest." [7]

"Accepting the definition of the Indian as less than human, William Bradford in 1620 considered New England to be uninhabited:"

"...the vast and unpeopled countries of America, which are fruitfull & Fitt for habitation, being devoyd of all civil inhabitants, where there are only savage & brutish men, which range up and downe, litle otherwise than the wild beasts of the same." [8]

John Smith urged the enslavement of the "viperous brood," which had earlier, he admitted, saved Jamestown from starvation. [9] Benjamin Trumbull held that "as Connecticut abounded in wild animals, so it did also with wild and savage men." [10] If Indians were defined as a kind of aninal, it was proper to hunt them as such, and bounties were offered for their scalps, just as for those of wolves.' 11 On the far western frontier in the nineteenth century, Indian flesh was eaten, like game.' 12

The view of the Indian as a wild beast in the path of civilization has never died. It was a dominant theme in the treatment of Indians by historians until quite recently. It still lurks in history books in phrases like "Indian menace," and "Indian peril," "savage barrier," and "obstacle to settlement."... One of the persistent faults in many historians is the inability to see that the whites were also a constant source of trouble to the Indians, and that the Indians, too, were often innocent victims of "cruel border warfare." 13 Not only are massacres of Indians generally overlooked, but also the fact that thousands of Indians were enslaved, some even being shipped to the Barbary States and the West Indies. 14 The "cruelty" stereotype of the Indian needs an examination it seldom gets. Cruelty there sometimes was, but in retaliation for cruelty inflicted, and then hardly worse than the tortures in vogue among whites of that time. 15 The many cases of white captives who were unwilling to return to "civilization" is an eloquent commentary on old images of the Indian. 16

Indian removal, or slaughter, is customarily presented as the inexorable march of civilization displacing savage hunters. Glyndon G. Van Deusen finds that the white invasion "was deeply resented by the red men, who saw their hunting grounds disappearing before these waves of intruders." 17 The "primitive hunter" myth is the usual expiation for the triumph of brute force. It appears repeatedly in the refrain that "the natives did not develop the land." We deplored the same logic when it was used by Mussolini in Ethiopia. If the right of ownership depended on land use, some wealthy white land owners would today be in jeopardy.

The myth of the Indian as a mere hunter, like many other myths, arises from ignorance concerning the variety of Indian cultures which flourished in America. Most Indians were farmers, and the Southeastern Indians had so far embraced "civilization" by the 1830s that they were known as the "Five Civilized Tribes." The Cherokee had adopted a constitution patterned after that of the United States, and published books and a newspaper in their own language, with Sequoyah's alphabet. A census taken among them in 1825 showed that they owned 33 grist mills, 13 saw mills, 1 powder mill, 69 blacksmith shops, 2 tan yards, 762 looms, 2486 spinning wheels, 172 wagons, 2923 plows, 7683 horses, 22,531 black cattle, 46,732 swine, and 2566 sheep.[18] This adaptation to white concepts of progress, urged upon them by Jefferson,[19] did not save them, but rather accelerated demands for their expulsion....

DEFAMATION

This school denigrates the Indian, calls attention to all of his faults and none of his virtues, and condemns him to a status of inferiority in intelligence and adaptability. To this group belongs John Bach McMaster, who may be taken as representative of the late nineteenth century historians. To him the Indian "was never so happy as when, in the dead of night, he roused his sleeping enemies with an unearthly yell, and massacred them by the light of their burning homes." The Indian was, moreover, only an "idle, shiftless savage." When not hunting or warring, he yielded himself to debauchery, and enslaved his women....

"IF YOU DON'T LIKE IT HERE IN AMERICA, WHY DON'T YOU GO BACK WHERE YOU CAME FROM?"

Reprinted by permission of the **Guardian**.

These historians are gone, but their influence is not. Their crude racism has gone out of fashion, but derogation of Indian character continues. In his Pulitzer prize-winning history, R. Carlyle Buley proclaims that "the Potawatomi and the Menominee were...a fairly dirty, lazy, and harmless lot." [20] The late David Saville Muzzey, whose books are widely used in high schools, promotes the myth of the nomadic warrior: (the Indians) "were constantly on the warpath, and shifting their hunting grounds." [21] The nomad myth is often used to deny the validity of Indian land claims. Most Indians were in fact less mobile than the current white population. [22] (How many of us were born where we now live?) The Mohawk village of Caughnawage, Que., is 300 years old this year. Tuscaloosa, Ala., was an Indian village when DeSoto came by in 1540. Oraibi, a Hopi village in Arizona, is the oldest continuously inhabited place in the United States. Tree ring evidence dates it back to 1100 A.D. Therefore, it is older than Berlin or Moscow.

The charge that all Indians were perpetual warriors arises from ascribing Plains Indian customs to all Indians. It is entirely inapplicable to the sedentary Pueblo tribes, and to some Pacific coast and Eastern woodland Indians as well. The role of Indians as peacemakers has been so hidden that a book has been written to rescue this aspect of their history from obscurity, but, like so many of the better books on Indians, it was the work of an "amateur." [23]

DISPARAGEMENT

The fourth way the Indian is scalped by historians is by **disparagement** of, or denial of his extensive contributions to our culture. Richard N. Current and his collaborators declare that "American civilization... owed very little to the aborigines of the New World." They further allege that "even the most brilliant of the native cultures were stunted in comparison with the growing civilization of Europe. None of the Indians had an alphabet and...none had any conception of the wheel." [24]

The last statement is false; the Aztecs used wheels on children's toys, but had no beasts of burden to enable them to put the principle to better use. But the

106

comparisons made above are perniciously unfair. Barbaric Europe borrowed its wheel and its alphabet, not to mention its numerals and many domesticated plants and animals, from Semitic peoples of Asia. Its gunpowder, compass, and printing press were inventions of Oriental people. Moreover, the argument ignores the instances in which American achievements exceeded those of the Old World: the Maya had a superior calendar and understood the zero before Europe did. Indians domesticated more than forty plants, of which corn is the outstanding example, because it does not and cannot grow wild. [25] In some respects, they excelled in medicine and surgery, e.g., transportation, and knew the properties of drugs like coca (from whence cocaine), cinchona (from whence quinine), curare, cascara sagrada, and many more. They alone discovered rubber, and with it invented the bulbed syringe. Middle American hieroglyphics, in time, would have evolved into an alphabet.

The remarks of Prof. Current also illustrate the selective criteria which are used to rank cultures into false categories called ''higher'' and ''lower.'' To measure social advance in **our** terms reveals an ethnocentric bias. This is ABC to an anthropologist, but not to all historians....

Even in areas where the Indian has made spectacular contributions, they are denied. Alden T. Vaughan alleges that ''the Indians had no bona fide medicine to speak of.'' [26] In fact, the Indians of North America (north of Mexico) used about 150 medicines which were later included in the **U.S. Pharmacopeia** and **National Formulary**, and the Indians of Latin America contributed about fifty more. [27] Accounts of explorers, from Cartier on, are filled with tributes to Indian medical skill which, although frequently mixed with magic, was considered by many to excel that of Europe at the time.

''Nor have the Indians made any sustantial contribution to the civilization that we now have in the United States,'' comments Oliver Perry Chitwood. [28] To be sure, he admits that the Indians aided the colonists at first. They taught colonists how to clear the land and grow corn and tobacco, acted as guides, procured furs for trade, taught the colonials how to make maple sugar, to hunt and trap, and dress their skins. They showed the white man how to make a bark canoe, and endowed our map with euphonious place names. Yet, he concludes, "aside from these contributions, American life has not been modified by Indian influence."...

The really comprehensive account of the Indian contributions remains to be written. What we have is mainly the work of anthropologists, and it is not always easily available. [29]

Let us take a closer look at the argument. Chitwood confines his attention to the aborigines of **our part** of this continent. Thus, not a nod or a footnote is accorded to the mighty attainments of the Middle American and Andean civilizations: the Mayan astronomy, mathematics, and architecture, the skillful metal work and other arts of the Aztecs and Incas, the domestication of the turkey, Muscovy duck, honeybee, alpaca, llama, and guinea pig; the roads, communications, scientific land use and political organization of the Incas; the invention of paper and the weaving of cotton cloth in Mexico, and other achievements previously mentioned. To judge Indian attainments by the more limited material progress of those living north of the Rio Grande is as one-sided as if we should measure European civlization by the achievements of the Lapps, or the primitive Germans described by Tacitus, or if we should subtract from Europe's culture all that was borrowed from Asia. [30]

Our Indians, it is said, failed to appreciate and exploit the resources at their disposal. This view fails to consider that the demographic facts caused no pressure for extensive development. Moreover, the Indian use of resources was different from ours. For example, the rivers and lakes were canoe routes and sources of food. We have turned them into foul sewers. The Plains were a hunting ground. There we overcultivated and turned the region into a dustbowl scarred by wind and rain. Recognizing no value in forests except as lumber, we cut them down and unleashed floods in our river valleys. We were so committed to the idea that all of nature's bounty should yield financial gain, that for a long time we failed to appreciate the recreational, ecological, and esthetic value of unspoiled wilderness. The concept of nature as an enemy to be slain lives on in the dogmas of Eric Hoffer. Belatedly we are returning some lands to their wild state, a retreat which would astonish our practical forefathers.

But North American Indians were not averse to resource development. They mined and worked copper, lead, mica, and coal. (Latin American Indians mined gold, silver, tin, platinum, and jade). They discovered oil and made salt by evaporation.[31] Southwestern Indians built irrigation canals, raised cotton, and farmed the land to a near optimum level. Where conditions permitted, North American Indians planted corn, squash, beans, pumpkins, tobacco, sunflowers, and drug plants. They discovered natural dyes which were used by the pioneers, and used hundreds of wild plants for food and medicine.

As Rome hid its debt to the Estruscans, we have obscured our inheritance from the red men. Anthropologists know that acculturation proceeds in both directions when two societies are in any kind of contact, and that even a conquered people helps to shape the destiny of their overlords. "North Americans have maintained the European level with the strictest possible puritanism," wrote psychiatrist Carl Jung, "yet they could not prevent the souls of their Indian enemies from becoming theirs."[32] For our own benefit, let us resurrect some lost truth.

FOOTNOTES

1 Parkman, **The Conspiracy of Pontiac** (New York: E. P. Dutton, 1908), II, 101.

2 Best accounts of the removal are Grant Foreman's two books, **Last Trek of the Indians** (Chicago: University of Chicago Press, 1946), which describes the expulsion of the Indians from the Old Northwest, and **Indian Removal** (Norman: University of Oklahoma Press, 1953), which deals with the Southern Indians. Also valuable for the latter is Dale Van Every, **The Disinherited** (New York: Avon Books, 1966).

3 **Autobiography of Black Hawk**, ed. by Donald Jackson (Urbana: University of Illinois Press, 1955).

4 Boston: Little Brown & Co., 1949.

5 Schlesinger does devote three sentences to the "case of the Georgia missionaries" (p. 350), as an example of how Jackson incurred the ire of religious groups, but says nothing about its effect on the Indians, and nothing about removal.

6 Mather in **Magnalia Christi Americana**, quoted in Alden T. Vaughan, **New England Frontier** (Boston: Little Brown & Co., 1965), p. 20.

7 Quoted in Jack D. Forbes, ed., **The Indian in America's Past** (Englewood Cliffs, N. J., Prentice-Hall, 1964), p. 113.

8 Bradford, **Of Plymouth Plantation** (New York: Capricorn Books, 1962), p. 40.

9 L. G. Tyler, ed., **Narratives of Early Virginia** (New York: Scribner's, 1907), pp. 37-41, 360, 364 ff. "Our provision being now within twentie dayes spent, the Indians brought us great store both of Corne and bread ready made," is one of several tributes Smith earlier paid to Indian generosity.

10 Trumbull, **A Complete History of Connecticut**, 1630-1764 (New London: H. D. Utley, 1898), p. 21.

11 On scalp bounties, see Emerson Hough, **The Passing of the Frontier** (New Haven: Yale University Press, 1893), pp. 134; Bancroft, **History**, I, 128-29; M. W. Stirling, **National Geographic Magazine**, November, 1937, p. 582; Beals, **American Earth**, p. 46; Daniel Boorstin, **The Americans, the National Experience** (New York: Random House, 1966) p. 127. Edward Channing relates that Leonard Calvert and his agent, Giles Brent, advised Maryland colonists to shoot all Indians on sight. (**History**, I, 259). On biological warfare, see Woodward, **A New American History**, p. 106.

12 Everett Dick, **Vanguards of the Frontier** (New York: D. Appleton Century, 1944), p. 511; Raymond W. Thorp and Robert Bunker, **Crow Killer** (New York: Signet, n.d.), p. 9.

13 E.g., the Conestoga, Gnadenhutten, and Sand Creek massacres. See Helen Hunt Jackson, **A Century of Dishonor** (New York: Harper Torchbooks, 1965), Chapters III, IX.

14 Almon W. Lauber, **Indian Slavery in Colonial Times** (New York: Columbia University Press, 1913).

15 In Montaigne's view "(we) surpass them in every kind of cruelty." Michel de Montaigne, **Complete Essays** (Stanford: Stanford University Press, 1958), p. 156.

16 See Cadwallader Colden, **The History of the Five Indian Nations** (Ithaca: Cornell University Press, 1964), pp. 180-81; William Smith, **Expedition Against the Ohio Indians** (Ann Arbor: University Microfilms, 1966), pp. 26-29.

17 Van Deusen, **The Jacksonian Era** (New York: Harper & Bros., 1959), p. 48.

18 Albert Gallatin, "Synopsis of Indian Tribes," in **Transactions and Collections of the American Antiquarian Society** (Cambridge, 1836), II, 157.

19 Address to chiefs of the Cherokee nation, January 10, 1806, in Adirenne Koch and William Peden, **The Life and Selected Writings of Thomas Jefferson** (New York: Modern Library, 1944), pp. 578-80.

20 Buley, **The Old Northwest** (2 vols.; Bloomington: University of Indiana Press, 1964), II, 127. **Cf.** the view of the Potawatoma by Pierre-Jean DeSmet, who reported in 1838 that he "had not seen so imposing a sight nor such fine-looking Indians in America." **Life, Letters and Travels of Father Pierre-Jean DeSmet, S.J.** (New York: Francis P. Harper, 1905), I, 157.

21 Muzzey, **A History of Our Country** (Boston: Ginn & Co., 1957), p. 24.

22 Henry Henshaw answered the "nomad" myth in his article "Popular Fallacies" in F. W. Hodge, ed., **Handbook of American Indians** (Bureau of American Ethnology, Bulletin 30, 2 vols.; Washington: Government Printing Office, 1907-10, II, 283.

23 Mabel Powers, **The Indian as Peacemaker** (New York: Fleming H. Revell Co., 1932).

24 Richard N. Current, T. Harry Williams, and Frank Freidel, **American History, A Survey** (2d ed.; New York: Alfred A. Knopf, 1966), p. 4.

25 Alphonse de Candolle, **The Origin of Cultivated Plants** (New York: D. Appleton & Co., 1902), **passim**.

26 Vaughan, **New England Frontier**, p. 34.

27 Virgil J. Vogel, ''American Indian Medicine and its Influence on White Medicine and Pharmacology,'' PhD dissertation, Department of History, University of Chicago, 1966. Abstract in **The Indian Historian**, December, 1967, pp. 12-15.

28 Chitwood, **A History of Colonial America** (New York: Harper & Bros., 1931), p. 19.

29 A good short statement is anthropologist A. Irving Hallowell's ''The Impact of the Indian on American Culture,'' in W. D. Wyman and C. B. Kroeber, eds., **The Frontier in Perspective** (Madison: University of Wisconsin Press, 1965), pp. 229-58. Much of the material presented herein is based on Hallowell's inquiry, or inspired by it.

30 Defending the Indians from the charge of ''lacking genius,'' Thomas Jefferson compared them with north Europeans at the time of Roman contact, and asked, ''how many good poets, how many able mathematicians, how many great inventors in arts or sciences, had Europe, north of the Alps, then produced? And it was sixteen centuries after this before a Newton could be formed.'' — ''Notes on Virginia,'' in Koch and Peden, **op cit.**, pp. 212-13.

31 C. A. Browne, ''The Chemical Industries of the American Aborigines,'' **Isis**, XXIII (1935), 406-24.

32 Jung, **Contributions to Analytical Psychology** (New York: Harcourt Brace & Co., 1928), p. 139.

THE "NOBLE SAVAGE" WASN'T ALL THAT NOBLE

John Greenway

John Greenway is a professor of anthropology at the University of Colorado in Boulder. The following article is excerpted from an essay-review of books on American Indians published by the **National Review**.

Use the following questions to assist your reading:

1. According to the author what was the real Indian like?
2. How does he describe the treatment of Indians in the U.S.?
3. What does he say about the Indian's relationship to democracy?
4. The author discusses the Indian as a "Victim" and the Indian as a "Litigant." What does he mean?

John Greenway, "Will the Indians Get Whitey?" **National Review**, March 11, 1969, pp. 223-28+. (c) National Review, Inc. 1969. Reprinted with permission. The editorial address of the **National Review** is (150 East 35 Street, New York, N.Y. 10016).

The unnatural eagerness of Americans to believe themselves to be monsters is not a biological imperative, despite its constancy from the earliest period of American history. It is learned behavior, implanted neither by genes nor by experience, but by the teachings of the strangest class of intellectuals any nation has ever been damned with. With few significant exceptions, America's professional thinkers have been anomic dropouts from their own culture, burning the American spirit as their bearded acolytes burn the American flag. They find some unrepented sin in themselves and take up whatever scourge lies at hand to visit its punishment upon their forefathers. Now more than ever before, the American Indian is a favorite scourge — as a study of ten popular, non-scholarly books[1] on the Indian demonstrates....

All of these books are stern indictments of Our Treatment of the Indians, though the authors have little more qualification to write books about the Indians than a plumber has to practice brain surgery.... They write about the Indian because the Indian in the American mind is as imaginary as Sandburg's Lincoln, a creation of fantasy, guilt and ignorance, on which everyone is his own authority. Edward Hicks should have painted the scene: in the background a massacre of Indian women and children; in the foreground a young Indian lad and his Indian lass, hand in hand, about to hurl themselves off a Lovers' Leap while singing ''By the Waters of Minnetonka.'' The illusion is always more romantic than the reality; in real life Running Bear would have been less likely to seduce little White Dove than to rape her.

The Indian As Dionysus

The lay reader should have a hardcore course in what the real Indian was like before exposing his raw conscience to books like these. He should know that the real Indian was ferocious, cruel, aggressive, stoic, violent, ultra-masculine, treacherous and warlike, though these are anemic adjectives to describe the extent of his Dionysiac extremism. As for Our Treatment of the Indians, never in the entire history of the inevitable displacement of hunting tribes by advanced agriculturists in the 39,000 generations of mankind has a native people been treated with more consideration, decency

113

and kindness. The Mongoloids in displacing the first comers of Asia, the Negroes in displacing the aborigines in Africa, and every other group following the biological law of the Competitive Exclusion Principle thought like the Polynesian chief who once observed to a white officer: ''I don't understand you English. You come here and take our land and then you spend the rest of your lives trying to make up for it. When my people came to these island, we just killed the inhabitants and that was the end of it.'' It could be argued that the only real injury the white man ever did the Indian was to take his fighting away from him. Indians did not fight to defend their land, their people or their honor, as these writers apparently believe; like the Irish, they fought for the fighting. Without war and raiding and scalping and rape and pillage and slave-taking, the Indian was as aimless as a chiropractor without a spine. There was nothing left in life for him but idleness, petty mischief and booze....

The Indian As Democrat

Our universities today swarm with men who truly believe that both the Constitution specifically and American democracy generally were copied from Indian originals. Some of these men have been seen to laugh at the New Fundamentalists for believing that Christ ascended to heaven in a space ship.

The Indians indeed did put up imitations of civilized institutions when it seemed profitable to do so, but they were the most palpable travesties. Dale Van Every's contribution to the Black Pages of White History, **Disinherited**, is an unintentional illustration of how academic folklore on the Indians is constructed. He meets the stringent standards of authority established by his peers, having once written a history entitled **The AEF in Battle** (which I have not read, fearing it might take the side of the Germans) and making movies for thirteen years. He deals with the central illusion, on which most of the others depend: that the Indians in the forest primeval were gathered into mighty nations. There were, he says, "twenty great Indian nations" in the Southeast alone, of which the greatest in civilization and suffering was the Cherokee. (Fact: From a population of two thousand in 1761, this great Cherokee empire was reduced by the white man's oppression, diseases, wars and massacres, to **fifty** thousand the last time they came into court to sue for the return of the Southeastern states.)

Within these nations pure democracy flourished. At the top of page 82 Mr. Van Every tells of the "instinctive sympathy" between Negroes and Indians, and of the "ingrained Indian abhorrence of slavery as an institution." At the bottom of page 82 Mr. Van Every gives us a census of the Cherokee Nation in 1825: 15,563 Indians; Negro slaves, 1,277. These were not refugee slaves; there were real slaves. In 1824 the Cherokee National Committee prohibited any of their Negroes from owning stock, voting or marrying Indians. Still, one must consider the iron law of economics; Van Every could make neither a book nor a movie on the Cherokee as they really were — intruders into the land the United States paid them for, important only because they were the victors in a bloody war to extermination or exile with other tribes — the Yamasee, Creek Choctaw, Shawnee, Catawba, Tuscarora and Chicasaw — over which tribe should have the monopoly of selling slaves to the South....

When Van Every's heart is not weeping for the Cherokee, it is hemorrhaging for the Seminoles, who established a claim to Florida that the Indian Claims Commission has offered to pay off in a 1965 decision. How did the Seminoles establish ownership to Florida? By fleeing over the Georgia line with Negro slaves they stole from the whites. The Seminoles have been granted a cash settlement for the state, but they still want the state. We may get off easy by giving them Miami....

The real Indian was only most tenuously a member of a tribe. His ecological unit was the nomadic band, either hunting-gathering or primitive agricultural, with little cohesion beyond an approximation to a common language and some weak psychological unity. These marauding social fragments cohered only when profitable raiding was visible.

Tribes have to have chiefs, so the white man invented that concept also. In the old days, the nearest any Indian tribe got to a chief was somebody who could persuade a few young braves to accompany him in a sneak raid on the neighbors' horses....

The Indian as Victim

When sneak attacks on horses escalated into massive and murderous raids on settlements, people would sometimes get hurt. But Washburn speaks for his peers when he forbids the term "massacre" to describe such incidents; such invidious expressions, he says, were designed to put the Indian into bad repute "and to provide good reason why he should be treated the way he was treated by that society." It is just as unfair, he adds, as accusing the Indian of cannibalism merely because he ate people.

116

So James C. Olson pours out his heart's blood for the Sioux in nearly 400 pages of **Red Cloud and the Sioux Problem** without ever finding it pertinent to mention the Minnesota Massacre, in which at least 800 whites were killed and 10,000 square miles of Minnesota cleared of settlers. About the only consistent use of the word "massacre" in these books appends to the Sand Creek and Wounded Knee massacres.[2]

It is, by the way, almost impossible to find a book giving the white side of the Sand Creek affair; authors ignore the voluminous testimony of the congressional investigation and accept the testimony instead of one Robert Bent, a survivor. This Bent makes an interesting witness; he was a renegade halfbreed who with his two brothers lived and raided with the Cheyenne. They were a precious trio; one of them captured a white settler, staked him to the ground, cut out his tongue, castrated him, and built a fire on his stomach.

In **The Long Death** Andrist mentions the Minnesota Massacre, but his interest is in the Indians who were captured, tried and executed for the murders — 39 Indians went to the gallows. Andrist (who is also the author of **Heroes of Polar Exploration**) chooses as the most regrettable part of the episode the second hanging of Rattling Runner, on whom the rope broke — "but the traditional ritual of legal life-taking had to be gone through in its entirety...his body was hoisted again, to dangle yet a while for the edification of the spectators." Rattling Runner's hangman, who so edified the crowd, had three children lying dead out on the plains, and his wife and two other children still in the tender hands of the uncaught Indians. Still, as the dustjacket judges, "Mr. Andrist writes with such passion that the reader hears the roar of guns and the rumble of hooves, the whistle of whips, the creak of wagon wheels, and always, and everywhere, the screams of dying and dis-possessed...the most fitting tribute ever written to the noblest victims Destiny ever had." The jacket is talking about the Indians....

Our books all stop short of the final subject in the sequence of Our Treatment of the Indian: the Indians' Treatment of Us. In 1960 the arrest rate for whites in the United States was 2,739 in 100,000. For Negroes it was 8,703. But for Indians it was 51,090. This inequity of iniquity has persuaded some racist commentators to

117

explain excessive criminality as a Mongoloid characteristic — but Chinese and Japanese in the United States
have the lowest arrest figure of any group, lower even
than for the most law-respecting WASPs....

The Indian As Litigant

As civilization displaces savagery, raiding becomes
litigation. The year of 1946 will be remembered not only
as the year ballpoint pens sold for $15.98, but as the
year the United States was given back to the Indians. It
was then that the Indian Claims Commission was
quietly established by Congress as a device to simplify
suits against the government for compensation for land
usurpation. In fact liability was admitted, with the only
issue to be determined in most cases being which
Indians should get the money. Five years were allowed
for the filing of claims, and by the 1951 deadine, 852
claims were entered for 70 per cent of the United
States.

This is not to say that the American conscience did
not awaken until 1946. Indians have been suing the
whites for more than a century.

Some Indians were paid as many as six times for the
same land, each time returning to complain that the
white man was an Indian giver.

And so from tribe to tribe (a tribe now is defined as
comprising any Indians the tribe council wishes to include in the loot). The Cherokee, who were themselves
invaders and usurpers of the land they occupied, have
received $14 million....

Their contending neighbors sued for $22 million and
settled for $1,769,940 in 1952. The Nex-Perce received
$3 million for their expenses in massacring settlers,
with their suit for 100,000 square miles of Idaho still in
litigation. Edmund Wilson's Seneca Nation was given
$12,128,917 out of court two years ago. The Utes got
$31,938,473.43 as a starter for the land they stole from
the Pueblos, and then made their expert anthro-
pological witness, Dr. Omer C. Stewart, wait nine
years for his $100-a-day fee (he was finally persuaded
to settle for half what was owed him).

An important point in this saga of masochistic largesse is how many Indians all this is going to....Altogether there are 550,000 Indians asking for $10 billion....

These claims do not include all the money going free from the taxpayer to the Indian. On the 397 federal reservations (eleven of which are over a million acres) no taxes are paid on...the land... And then there are the continuing service subsidies from the Bureau of Indian Affairs — $221,482,405 in the last official report, with many more millions hidden in other areas of budgetry....

How far can it all go? Will the 22 million Negroes in the United States sue the Government for all that free labor before 1865? Will the descendants of Adam enter a claim against the United States (God being safely dead) for their ancestor's unjust expulsion from the Garden?... Will the Americans ever find out where to go to surrender for the crime of being Americans?...

FOOTNOTES

1 **The Long Death: The Last Days of the Plains Indians,** by Ralph K. Andrist, Macmillan, $8.95. **The Flight of the Nez Perce: A History of the Nez Perce War** by Mark H. Brown. Putnam, $8.95. **The Shoshoneans: The People of the Basin-Plateau** by Edward Dorn and Leroy Lucas. Morrow, $6.95. **Warriors of the Colorado: The Yumas of the Quechan Nation and their Neighbors** by Jack D. Forbes. Oklahoma, $5.95. **The Nez Perce Indians and the Opening of the Northwest** by Alven M. Josephy Jr. Yale, $12.50. **Red Cloud and the Sioux Problem** by James C. Olson. Nebraska, $5.95. **Half Sun on the Columbia: A Biography of Chief Moses** by Robert H. Ruby and John H. Brown. Oklahoma, $5.95. **Disinherited: The Lost Birthright of the American Indian** by Dale Van Every. Morrow, $ .95 (paper). **The Indian and the White Man** by Wilcomb E. Washburn. Doubleday Anchor, $1.95 (paper). **Apologies to the Iroquois,** by Edmund Wilson. Random House, $1.95 (paper).

2 A typical distortion of the facts. The assemblage of Indians at Wounded Knee were hostiles dancing the Ghost Dance, which among the Sioux demanded genocide of the whites. The fighting — which indeed ended with the total slaughter of the Indians by soldiers harboring long infuriation for unavenged killings by the Indians — began when a shaman blew the eagle whistle and Indians pulled concealed rifles from under their blankets. The Wounded Knee Massacre put an end to Indian wars.

EXERCISE 6

LOCATING SCAPEGOATS

Instructions

The word fascism has emotional and controversial overtones. Scholars often disagree about its meaning. It conjures up images of Hitler, the swastika and Nazi horrors. During their occupation of Europe in the 1940's, the German fascists systematically killed an estimated six million Jews. They continually propagandized the outrageous lie that Jews were responsible for Germany's social ills and problems. Jews became scapegoats of irrational leaders who glorified force, violence, and the doctrines of racial supremacy. The fascists destroyed German democracy by adopting tactics of deceit and propaganda.

THE WHITE MAN'S BURDEN

Christian Vanguard, June, 1973.

One of their principal propaganda weapons was the technique of scapegoating. On an individual level scapegoating involves the mental process of transferring personal blame or anger to another individual or object. Most people, for example, have kicked their table or chair as a psychological outlet for anger and frustration over a mistake or failure. On a social level, this process involves the placement of blame on entire groups of people for social problems that they have not caused. Scapegoats may be totally or only partially innocent, but they always receive more blame than can be rationally justified.

121

Human societies are so complex that complicated problems are often not completely understood by any citizen. Yet people always demand answers and there exists a human tendency to create imaginary and simplistic explanations for complex racial, social, economic, and political problems that defy easy understanding and solution. In times of great social turmoil, people are more prone to accept the conspiratorial ideas of those who preach hate and unreason. Conspiracy theories of history and causation represent the most dangerous form of scapegoating. This social phenomenon occurs when racial, religious, or ethnic groups are unjustly blamed for serious social problems. This blame can be expressed in terms of verbal and/or overt hatred and aggression. Although scapegoating was a major tactic of the German fascists under Hitler, it is a commonly used technique of contemporary racists and fascists in America. The following activity is designed to help you understand this technique.

Part I

The above cartoon is an example of scapegoating. Examine the cartoon carefully and, with other class members, discuss why it is an example of scapegoating.

Part II

Read through the following list carefully. Some of the statements are taken from the readings in Chapter Three. Mark (S) for any statement that is an example of scapegoating. Mark (N) for any statement that is not an example of scapegoating. Mark (U) if you are undecided about any statement. Then discuss and compare your decisions with other class members.

S = An Example of Scapegoating
N = Not an Example
U = Undecided

_____ 1. School busing to promote integration causes social conflict and polarizes the community.

_____ 2. Only by ending capitalism can we stop the oppression of women in American society.

_____3. Did you know that the people commonly called Jews by most Christians are in reality the very synagogue of Satan?

_____4. The Nordic peoples are a superior race and have been largely responsible for the world's great achievements.

_____5. The real Indian was ferocious, cruel, aggressive, stoic, violent, ultramasculine, treacherous, and warlike.

_____6. If blacks are elected to the city council and take over the city government, the streets will not be safe and crime will cause whites to flee.

_____7. Equal Rights Amendment proponents have failed to make a case that a constitutional amendment is needed to promote women's rights.

_____8. The idea of the Indian as a wild beast in the path of civilization has never died.

_____9. On the western frontier in the nineteenth century, Indians were thought of as wild animals and hunted like game. Bounties were offered for their scalps.

_____10. The Equal Rights Amendment will help women gain their rights in a sexist society.

_____11. Without war and raiding and scalping and rape and pillage and slavetaking, the Indian was as aimless as a chiropractor without a spine.

_____12. The choice for courageous national leadership should be to support busing to integrate schools and not to pander to national fears and hysteria.

4 CHAPTER

JUSTICE AND FOREIGN POLICY

CHILEAN INTERVENTION VIOLATES AMERICAN VALUES

Robert C. Johansen

Robert C. Johansen is a professor of political science at Manchester College. He wrote the following article while he was a visiting research fellow at the Center of International Studies, Princeton University.

The following questions should help you examine the reading:

1. According to the author, why did the Nixon administration intervene in Chile?
2. What is political pluralism and how does the author say our intervention in Chile damages political pluralism?
3. Why does the author say our intervention in Chile damages U.S. security, works against Chilean interests, and weakens American democracy?
4. How does he say our foreign policy should be changed?
5. Can you relate the cartoons in this reading to the author's ideas?

Robert C. Johansen "Value Contradictions in U.S. Foreign Policy," **The Christian Century**, April 2, 1975, pp. 328-32. Copyright 1975 Christian Century Foundation. Reprinted by permission from the April 2, 1975 issue of **The Christian Century**.

The CIA's surreptitious stimulation of civil strife in Chile illustrates a tragic flaw in United States foreign policy: the acute incongruity between the articulated goals of policy and the means used to implement policy. In other words, instrumental values contradict goal values. Recognizing this contradiction can help us understand the conflict between the defenders and the critics of American foreign policy. The defenders generally focus on goals, which may on an abstract level seem defensible; opponents focus on the human suffering and injustice that flow from the means adopted to implement policy goals.

Examining Means and Ends

From the moment that Marxist physician Salvador Allende Gossens was elected president of Chile in a legal and free election, Washington officials showed their displeasure. They promised, however, not to intervene in the affairs of the Chilean people, who had expressed themselves at the ballot box. In September, 1973, after months of strike activity and rising economic discontent in Chile, Allende died during a violent military takeover of his government. Washington officials soon expressed their pleasure at the collapse of the Allende administration by extending recognition and financial assistance to the new dictatorship.

From the time of Allende's election until his death, rumors flourished about possible U.S. intervention in Chile. All rumors were officially denied. In truth — or as much truth as investigators have with difficulty been able to ferret out — the CIA played a substantial role in creating conditions designed to ensure a speedy overthrow of the elected government. When in October 1970 the Chilean congress ratified Allende's electoral victory, the U.S. Department of State solemnly told the American people that the U.S. had "firmly rejected" any attempt to block his inauguration. But in fact $350,000 had been secretly authorized earlier for an unsuccessful effort to bribe members of the Chilean congress to prevent Allende's inauguration.

As **New York Times** correspondent Seymour Hersh reported, CIA Director William F. Colby told a congressional committee in secret testimony that the CIA had intervened against Allende first in 1964, during the Johnson administration, to influence the outcome of an earlier election.

After Allende's election, the Nixon administration authorized an expenditure of $8 million for covert efforts to ''destabilize'' Chilean society and to make it impossible for elected Chilean officials to govern. If these efforts succeeded in polarizing political forces in Chile, then the apparent U.S. goals would be achieved: (1) to prove that a Marxist could not govern within a democratic, constitutional framework, and (2) thereby to discourage radical socio-economic change, in Chile and elsewhere, that was inimical to U.S. economic advantage and political hegemony....

CHILE!

Ollie Harrington in **The Daily World**, reprinted by permission

What 'Political Pluralism' Covers

Can the values implicit in the U.S. government's activities in Chile reasonably be expected to further the articulated goals of foreign policy? If there are contradictions between values implicit in the means and the goals as officially stated, what end values are actually served by those means? In order to answer these questions, let me compare the four explicit justifications of American policy with the implicit values of the means.

Professed value I: to protect political pluralism. Despite the statements of Secretary Kissinger and President Ford, the bulk of the secret money went to finance strikes and clandestine, destabilizing activity in Chile; it was not used to promote political pluralism. Less than half the funds were used for direct support of the allegedly threatened politicians, newspapers, and radio and television stations. One official explained that support for the media was necessary not because the United States wanted to preserve opposition media for their own sake — the CIA has not generally encouraged opposition media in dictatorships of the right — but because "it wouldn't have been good to have strikes if nobody knows about it."

It was not the official values but rather an alternative set of values that was embedded in the secret operations:

Implicit value A: to undermine the principle of self-determination. The United States violated the right of Chileans to govern themselves. Washington not only opposed self-determination but actively worked to subvert a legal election. By so doing, U.S. officials helped destroy political pluralism, civil liberties and democracy in Chile, fragile though their existence may have been. Certainly their fragility resulted as much from decades of U.S. dominance of Latin American politics as from the Allende regime itself.

Implicit value B: to encourage conditions likely to produce civil strife and violence. The United States violated its pledge to refrain from fostering a climate conducive to violence. The coup that was encouraged by U.S. involvement brought with it much bloodshed: several thousand persons were killed and untold thousands were arbitrarily arrested and tortured. A harsh new dictatorship shackled the press, prohibited activity by political parties, forced the closing of the congress, and abrogated civil liberties.

Damaging U.S. Security

Professed value II: to protect United States national security. The existence of the Allende government in itself could hardly have threatened U.S. security. Allende had no plans to attack the U.S. or to harm or subvert any neighboring states. If Allende's government was regarded in official minds as a threat, it could only have been because of his efforts to provide an electoral approach to the radical redistribution of wealth and power in a Latin American society. If such an approach could succeed in Chile, perhaps it would appeal elsewhere. By acting as if such an event constituted a threat to U.S. security, Kissinger, Nixon and Ford have sided with the forces of privilege, economic exploitation, repression and injustice.

In invoking national security, Ford was presumably falling back on cold-war cliches to justify the CIA operation as part of a general policy of opposition to communism. Curiously, in justifying the clandestine intervention, Ford revealed how much even in his own mind the guiding principle — if not the dollar cost — of United States foreign policy is similar to that of Soviet policy: "Communist nations spend vastly more money than we do for the **same kind of purposes**" (emphasis added).

If the national security argument is also an improbable justification for U.S. policy, what impact on security resulted from such clandestine intervention?

Implicit value: to damage United States security in the long run. The policy of secret intervention encourages other nations, including adversaries of the U.S., to employ "dirty tricks" even more widely. These actions victimize small societies, subject them to great power machinations, and make orderly, humane change less likely. Reformers learn either to accept the status quo or to become revolutionaries.

Such intervention creates an image throughout the

world of the U.S. as a manipulative, unfair, dishonest, ruthless giant trampling on the rights of the weak and poor. At the time of the Chilean revelations, Daniel Patrick Moynihan, U.S. ambassador to India, noted this effect in that country. Washington's posture leads other nations to blame the U.S. even for some subversion of which it is innocent. In the long run this image of the United States can hardly serve the legitimate security needs of any American citizen.

A policy of intervention lowers expectations for legal behavior in the international community. It is foolish, of course, to believe that if the CIA ceased interventions the Soviet KGB would immediately stop them also, but it is equally foolish to ignore the reality that norms of behavior do influence decisionmakers, and the norms themselves are strengthened or weakened by the U.S. government's behavior. When President Ford and other officials justify American intervention on the grounds that the U.S.S.R. also does it, they thereby encourage a gradual deterioration of expectations about what constitutes conventional, legitimate international behavior. That lowering of expectations jeopardizes the security not merely of all Americans but of all who live on this planet.

TORTURE UNDER CHILE'S JUNTA

Tales of savagery toward children; the torture of parents and children in each other's presence; reports by imprisoned women forced to watch the slow, systematic death-by-torture of young men whose hands and feet were cut off, eyes gouged out between beatings, and the programs designed to manipulate young minds continued to shock us.

Amnesty Action, May, 1975, p. 1.

Interventionism distracts decision-makers from the task of constructing foreign policies that deal with root causes of international problems. The CIA intervention in Chile is only the most recent example of U.S. refusal to allow, let alone to assist, foreign political leadership to reallocate wealth and power in order to provide for minimal human needs in societies bloated with misery....

Working Against Chilean Interests

Professed value III: to protect the interests of the Chilean people. President Ford did not specify what Chilean interests were protected by American intervention, but presumably he had in mind, in addition to political pluralism, the protection of private investment and private profit as a guiding principle for Chile's most needy citizens. In addition, American policy had other negative effects:

Implicit value A: to prevent the exercise of self-determination in Chile (as noted previously).

Implicit value B: to discourage the rule of law and the growth of respect for fair, humane processes of social change. At the same time that American policy brought violence and repression to Chile, it mocked moderate reformers who genuinely believed that the United States would not subvert Chile's legal processes.

Implicit value C: to encourage corruption of Chilean officials. Bribery is a constitutionally defined ground for impeachment in the United States, but in Chile the U.S. sought to bribe political leaders and then to enthrone those successfully bribed.

Implicit value D: to discourage Chilean elites from solving their domestic problems of injustice and human suffering. Ruling elites, such as the Chilean dictatorship, are invited to focus on relations with the United States and to enrich a small elite of pro-American collaborators, meanwhile ignoring the legitimate grievances of the vast majority of people. The regime's hold on power, after all, depends as much on maintaining friendly relations with the United States as it does on meeting grievances of its own people.

131

Andrews in **The Daily World**, reprinted by permission.

Implicit value E: to discourage elites from dealing with the international dimensions of their internal problems. Ruling elites are reluctant to examine the extent to which the poverty of their suppressed classes is due to the wealth of the United States and of pro-American collaborators within their own societies. The preoccupation of Latin American govenments with bilateral relations with the United States prevents them from recognizing the necessity of moving the international political structure into phase with the functional unity required to serve the human needs of the planet. They fail to press for systemic change in the global structure that would facilitate the reallocation of the world's wealth and authority. Instead they remain content with their privileged position in a national structure propped up by the CIA.

Weakening U.S. Democracy

Professed value IV: to protect the interests (in addition to security) of the American people. The only likely U.S. beneficiaries of the intervention were the owners of American corporations in Chile. They, of course, opposed self-determination for Chile. Ironically, many non-Marxist Chilean leaders as well as Marxists favored expropriation of certain U.S. companies. Thus, in the long run, it is probable that only significant U.S. manipulation of Chilean politics, continued indefinitely, can prevent growing Chilean control over American corporations.

Despite President Ford's assurance that intervention benefits most American citizens, the values implicit in the means of intervention violate the interests of the American people.

Implicit value A: to undermine the legitimacy of the United States government within American society. Secret CIA activity abroad spills over into illegal governmental behavior at home. The Pentagon Papers and Watergate provide ample evidence that decision-makers who develop strategies to subvert self-determination abroad are tempted to subvert it at home as well. As Daniel Ellsberg said after the first Watergate revelations, the logic of Watergate was the same as the logic of the U.S. government's Vietnamese policy, as documented in the Pentagon Papers: for U.S. officials, the law stops at the White House fence. As in Chile, Washington officials saw themselves as being above the law; it was no accident that the cover-up of Watergate was based on phony claims of national security and CIA secrets.

Implicit value B: to destroy the fabric of democracy within the United States. CIA operations lower the expectations of citizens that their government will be honest and open. If "dirty tricks" are carried out, officials will inevitably lie about them. When accurate information is no longer available or highly valued in a society, the practice of democracy becomes impossible.

133

The government's very insistence on the need for secrecy indicates that it does not welcome citizen participation in decision-making. In this sense Washington national security managers have become enemies of the people....

Needed: A Global System

An imperative for our troubled planet is to bring the instruments of U.S. policy into line with policy ends and to make ends serve global human needs, rather than the accumulation of national or personal power by U.S. officials. In the case of Chile, the instruments of United States policy did not and could not lead to desirable ends. To make national policies responsive to global human needs requires re-examination of our highest values and reorientation of American policy....

None of the values of human dignity can be satisfactorily served by individual nation-states acting separately, even assuming their goodwill. For example, the simple exercise of national sovereignty by a superpower violates the principle of global self-determination; any important policy of the United States affects millions of co-inhabitants of the globe who are, because of national divisions of the planet, unrepresented in the American policy process. A dispersal of power at the national level through an augmentation of authority at the world and subnational levels is required to provide an effective, central planetary guidance system to minimize violence, to coordinate supplies of scarce resources, to enhance human rights, and to promote human welfare on a global basis.

AMERICAN INTERVENTION IN CHILE WAS JUSTIFIED

Fred Schwarz

Dr. Fred Schwarz quit his medical practice in Sydney, Australia, and devoted himself to opposing Communism. He has traveled the world over, warning people about what he considers to be the dangers of Communism. In 1953 he organized the Christian Anti-Communism Crusade. This organization distributes literature and holds seminars about the threat of Communism. The headquarters of the Christian Anti-Communism Crusade is in Long Beach California.

Bring the following questions to your reading:

1. According to the author, what was the extent of CIA involvement in Chile? Why does he justify the involvement?
2. What does he say was most responsible for the defeat of the Allende government in Chile?
3. Why does the author prefer the present military dictatorship in Chile to the Communist government of Salvador Allende?

Fred Schwarz, ''Chile, the CIA and Communism,'' **Christian Anti-Communism Crusade**, November 1, 1974, pp. 1-4.

The cries of outraged protest with which many congressmen and community leaders have responded to the allegation that the C.I.A. spent $11 million to support opponents of the socialist-communist government of Chile reveal the transformed attitude towards international communism which prevails today.

Two important questions arise:

1. Is it permissible for agencies of the United States government to take educational and economic measures to prevent the establishment of a communist dictatorship in the Western Hemisphere?

2. Is it permissible to consider probable future developments as well as existing conditions in determining national policy?

1. Consequences of Communist Dictatorship in Chile:

The establishment of a communist dictatorship in Chile would be a threat to the military security of the U.S.A. as well as to the personal freedom of its citizens. This may seem an extreme statement but it is true. Communism is like a cancerous lesion that will not be satisfied until it has penetrated the body politic of the entire world. Communist leaders have repeatedly stated this. During the past two years, the inevitability of communist conquest has been reaffirmed by the communist leaders of the Soviet Union and Communist China.

Communism rules a country through the Dictatorship of the Communist Party which is incorrectly called the Dictatorship of the Proletariat. The elite majority, which comprises the communist party, seizes and retains all the sources of power. It creates and controls its own army and police force which it substitutes for the former army and police. It legislates, adjudicates, and administers while controlling the entire economy. The citizens are reduced to slaves who receive their food, education, and right to live at the discretion of the communist party. The triumph of communism is a tragedy for the people of any nation.

Once a country is conquered by communism, it becomes a stepping stone for the conquest of neighboring countries. The communist conquest of Cuba provided the Soviet Union with a base from which missiles could threaten major cities of the United States. This brought the world to the brink of thermonuclear war during the Cuban missile crisis. The establishment of an additional communist base in Chile would have presented immediate threats to other countries in South America and ultimately to the United States.

It has long been accepted that one of the functions of the American Government is to protect the American people from external communist aggression. President John Kennedy stated that the existence of a communist regime in the western hemisphere was intolerable. How would he have described the existence of two communist regimes?

CLANDESTINE EFFORTS?

It may be that interference of any kind in the affairs of another country should be discouraged. But is it really a purely Chilean "affair" if it is contemplated that hundreds of millions of dollars of American investments are to be confiscated? Is it purely a Chilean affair if the country becomes a base for revolutionary activities against its neighbors?

What if a country's government is being arrantly subsidized by the Soviet Union? Is it then — and only then — a responsibility of the United States to grant countervailing aid? Are we in fact prepared to retreat so completely from the inaugural ideal of John F. Kennedy ("We shall pay any price, bear any burden, meet any hardship, support any friend, oppose any foe, in order to assure the survival and the success of liberty...") as to stop any clandestine effort to help our friends in other countries to help themselves?

William F. Buckley, "The CIA In Chile," **National Review**.

The use of educational and economic measures to influence the internal policies of other countries is an accepted and legitimate governmental function. For example, the Senate of the United States, under the

137

leadership of Senator Henry Jackson of Washington State, recently voted to deny "most favored nation" trading relations to the Soviet Union because of its treatment of Soviet Jews and other minority groups.

As a result of the economic pressure thus applied, the Soviet Union has agreed to liberalize its immigration policies for its Jewish citizens. This is a blatant example of the use of economic pressures to influence governmental policies of other nations, but most members of Congress seem to applaud it. It is accepted international procedure.

The Soviet Union spends $1½ million a day to sustain the communist government of Cuba. It spends vast sums on literature and radio propaganda to influence public opinion in the United States. Must the United States do nothing when a neighbor is threatened by communism?

The sums of money allegedly distributed by the C.I.A. during several years in Chile were modest indeed when compared with typical governmental expenditures. The purpose of their expenditure was to preserve the democratic process in Chile. There is no vestige of evidence that the C.I.A. organized or supported the military coup which overthrew Allende.

2. Progress Towards Communist Dictatorship:

The statement is repeatedly made that the Allende Government was operating through the democratic process and that the overthrow of Allende was the overthrow of democracy in Chile. This is like claiming that in 1932 the Hitler Government was operating through the democratic process and that the overthrow of the Hitler regime would have been the destruction of democracy in Germany.

Such statements ignore the fact that policies change as conditions change. In communist jargon it is to view a situation statically instead of dialectically. Intelligent actions demand consideration of the probable future as well as the present. The future can only be predicted by giving attention to the ideology and intentions of the rulers.

The Allende Government represented a coalition

known as the Popular Unity. The principle parties in the coalition were the communist and the socialist parties. Both of these parties were radical revolutionary parties determined to establish "socialism" in Chile. Socialism was defined in the Marxist-Leninist sense as government by the dictatorship of the proletariat. They repeatedly affirmed that "socialism" had not yet been established in Chile and that they had chosen the democratic pathway to socialism. This meant that they would utilize the democratic institutions of society in order to become strong enough to destroy them and replace them by "socialist" institutions. Such institutions would include: Workers Committees (Soviets) to replace Congress and a Red Army to replace the Chilean Army. Both the Soviets and the Red Army existed in embryonic form at the time the Chilean military seized power. Industrial cordones consisting of worker-representatives from industries which had been seized could easily have been transformed into Soviets

139

and workers defense forces into the Red Army. Reports from communist sources claimed that half a million Chilean workers had been armed and Chile was confronted with a civil war which would probably have been comparable to the Spanish civil war when the army launched its coup.

Any American policy which did not take potential developments into consideration would have been puerile and irresponsible.

The influence of the C.I.A. in the events that took place in Chile was minimal. This is the verdict of the communist leaders as they review the events that led up to the military coup itself. The WORLD MARXIST REVIEW of July, 1974, publishes a letter from Rene Castillo, Member of the Leadership of the Communist Party of Chile which analyzes the reasons for the defeat of the Popular Unity. Castillo places the blame for this defeat primarily upon mistakes made by the leaders and on conflicts between the parties. He states:

"When power is won without armed struggle the ruling classes naturally seek to take advantage of 'legality' in their fight against the revolution. But this is the same 'legality' which justifies the revolutionary government in the eyes of broad sections of the public. It becomes a factor in facilitating, to a certain degree, revolutionary change and the marshalling of forces. **Insofar as this is a transitional stage, the old government institutions are temporarily retained.** But the revolutionary movement should not lose sight of the fact that the democratic institutions inherited from the old system are of a class nature, and democratic development inevitably entails changing the class character of the state. That is the only way to assure the advance of the revolution. The enemy tries to exploit the situation by using government institutions where he still dominates to do away with those which no longer promote his class domination. This is where our government made a number of mistakes, which enabled the reactionaries to take advantage of democratic freedoms to create conditions for a fascist **coup d'etat**, doing away with democracy altogether." (Pages 86-87)

Particular attention should be paid to this statement that Chile was in a transitional stage and that the retention of the old government institutions, e.g. Congress, was temporary.

Disunity Between Communists and Socialists

He blames disunity between the communist and socialist parties for causing the defeat:

"The Popular Unity parties and movements believe that the defeat was due mainly to the absence of a united leadership pursuing a principled policy and avoiding the pitfalls of 'Left' and 'Right' opportunist deviations. In this respect solid unity of Socialists and Communists is decisive.

"In Chile, Socialist-Communist unity goes back 20 years... Of course, there were difficulties... In the crucible of the class struggle that followed the people's victory, they made themselves more painfully felt.

"The Communist Party of Chile is a working class party. However, our leadership of the proletariat and the people and the fulfilment of our vanguard role presuppose cooperation with the Socialist Party, which likewise has important positions among the working people... We discussed matters at leadership level and explained our class position. But we were not doing enough at local branch level, among the people. And yet such work could have prevented the spread of petty-bourgeois revolution which militated against Socialist-Communist unity and the revolutionary process as a whole." (Pages 88 and 89)

Political Defeat

He acknowledges that they were defeated politically in Chile before the military defeat:

"Though our policy won wide acceptance and though a substantial part of the working class and the people worked with dedication to achieve the goals of the revolution, we were not able to unite the whole popular movement on this basis.

"Indeed, the Popular Unity was unable to prevent isolation of the working class or to win over the majority

of the population, whose vital interests were insepa-
rably linked with the success of the popular government. This predetermined the victory of counter-re-
volution in the battle for power. We suffered both
military and political defeat (military defeat was due
mainly to our political defeat). We were defeated
because the working class was isolated from its allies.

"And it is in this sense that **we assess our defeat
primarily as a political one** and only after that as a
military one. The isolation of the working class from its
allies enabled the reactionaries to launch their coup.
Isolation ruled out the possibility of the working class
and the people taking up arms. We officially state that
there could have been such a possibility, but only if it
were not tantamount to mass suicide." (Pages 93 and
94)

The communist movement is an international movement. Since the overthrow of the Allende regime in
Chile, the communist propaganda apparatus has
carried on a persistent campaign to present a false
picture of the events in Chile. The Allende regime has
been presented as the essence of pure democracy while
the military leadership is portrayed as consisting of
cruel murdering fascists without redeeming qualities.
Every communist periodical carries articles attacking
the junta in Chile. It is a rare edition of the **Daily World**
that does not contain several articles. It is difficult to
avoid admiration for the perseverance of the communist
propagandists and their campaign is now bearing fruit.

We must hope and work for the creation of economic
well-being and personal liberty in Chile. Both of these
would have been denied permanently by the triumph of
communism in that country.

EXERCISE **7**

RECOGNIZING ETHNOCENTRIC STATEMENTS

PART I

Instructions

Ethnocentrism is the tendency for people to feel their race, religion, culture, or nation is superior and to judge others by one's own frame of reference. **Frame of reference** means the standards and values a person accepts because of his life experience and culture. A Marxist in Russia, for example, is likely to view things differently than a Christian in France.

143

Ethnocentrism has promoted much misunderstanding and conflict. It helps emphasize cultural differences and the notion that your nation's institutions are superior. Education, however, should stress the similarities of the human condition throughout the world and the basic equality and dignity of all men.

In order to avoid war and violence, people must realize how **ethnocentrism** and **frame of reference** limit their ability to be objective and understanding. Consider each of the following statements carefully. Mark (**E**) for any statements you think is ethnocentric. Mark (**N**) for any statement you think is not ethnocentric. Mark (**U**) if you are undecided about any statement.

E = **Ethnocentric**
N = **Not Ethnocentric**
U = **Undecided**

_____1. The countries of the world should promote economic cooperation rather than competition.

_____2. Only Americans can lead the world to the path of peace and prosperity.

_____3. People in Europe and Africa have many things in common.

_____4. Native Americans discovered Columbus as he was about to land on their shore.

_____5. Columbus did not know that he had discovered a new world.

_____6. Columbus discovered America.

_____7. The Indians were often unfriendly toward settlers on the western frontier.

_____8. Many people have been influenced by Christianity.

_____9. America's achievements are more remarkable than those of other countries.

_____10. The urban crisis is one of America's most serious problems.

_____11. American military involvement in the Indochina War was an example of arrogance and misuse of power.

_____12. If the world can act toward China with generosity and understanding, it will be on the way to a solution of the great problems of Asia.

_____13. Americans should not act as the world's policeman.

_____14. God has been preparing the English-speaking peoples for a thousand years to be the master organizers of the world.

_____15. Education should stress the essential similarities of the human condition.

SELECTED PERIODICAL BIBLIOGRAPHY

The editor has compiled a periodical bibliography. For the student's convenience, it is organized into four topical areas that relate to the four chapters in the text. It is hoped that the following titles will be helpful to students searching for more information about the issues presented in this book.

CRIMINAL JUSTICE

"A Bill of Impeachment," **The Progressive**, December, 1973, pp. 4-5.

Buckley, William F., "Let Him Go," **National Review**, August 30, 1974, p. 995.

Buckley, William F., "The Kidnapper," **National Review**, June 7, 1974, p. 664.

Buckley, William F., "The Prisoner of San Clemente," **National Review**, September 13, 1974, p. 1060.

Gazzaniga, Michael, "The Marijuana Business," **National Review**, June 6, 1975, pp. 610-11.

Graham, Richard W., "The Narcotics Project," **The New Republic**, February 1, 1974, pp. 14-17.

Howard, Phillips, "Helms Only Senator Against Youth Crime Bill," **Human Events**, August 17, 1974, p. 8.

"Justice in Jeopardy," **The Progressive**, March, 1975, p. 7.

Kilpatrick, James J., "Criminal Justice System a Dismal and Tragic Failure," **Human Events**, May 10, 1975, p. 9.

Kilpatrick, James J., "The Way to Reduce Crime," **Nation's Business**, April, 1975, p. 7.

Kirk, Russell, "Juveniles in Trouble," **National Review**, October 25, 1974, p. 1241.

Lewis, Anthony, "An Agenda for Justice," **The New Republic**, February 8, 1975, pp. 15-18.

Lofton, John D. Jr., "Looking Up Criminals is One Cure for Crime," **Human Events**, May 24, 1975, p. 12.

Mackenzie, John P., "Judging the Judiciary," **The Progressive**, August, 1974, pp. 18-21.

Matthews, John, "The Supreme Court on Students' Rights," **The New Republic**, March 29, 1975, pp. 16-17.

Miller, Arthur S., "Watergate and Beyond: The Issue is Secrecy," **The Progressive**, December, 1973, pp. 15-19.

Nathan, Robert Stuart, and Norma Levy, "Specializing the Law," **The New Republic**, April 26, 1975, pp. 5-6.

Roberts, Michael, "Give 'em Death?" **The New Republic**, April 19, 1975, pp. 17-19.

TRB from Washington, "Denying the Obvious," **The New Republic**, April 12, 1975, p. 2.

"Tough Words on Crime by L.A. Police Chief," **Human Events**, March 22, 1975, p. 8.

"Watergatism," **National Review**, November 22, 1974, p. 1341.

Wells, Charles A., "Amnesty and the President," **Between the Lines**, October 1, 1974, p. 3.

ECONOMIC JUSTICE

Agran, Larry, "Getting Cancer on the Job," **The Nation**, April 12, 1975, pp. 433-37.

"American Military Power Sliding into Second Place," **U.S. News & World Report**, November 4, 1974, pp. 30-32.

Barnes, Peter, "Bringing Back the WPA," **The New Republic**, March 15, 1975, pp. 19-21.

Barnes, Peter, "Who'll Control Sun Power?" **The New Republic**, February 1, 1975, pp. 17-19.

Barnes, Peter and Derek Shearer, "Beyond Anti-Trust," **The New Republic**, July 6 & 13, 1974, pp. 17-19.

Boyte, Harry, "Prospectus for a New Party," **The Progressive**, July, 1974, pp. 13-18.

Brownfeld, Allan, "Anti-Defense Lobby Misleads Public," **Human Events**, March 1, 1975, p. 9.

Byron, William J., "Seeking a Just Society: An Agenda for Americans," **America**, March 29, 1975, pp. 229-33.

Chapman, William, "The Housing Hustlers," **The Progressive**, May, 1974, pp. 29-32.

"Charles H. Smith Jr. of SIFCO Industries Interviewed on Multinational Corporations," **Nation's Business**, May, 1974, pp. 42-46.

Coase, R.H., "The Market for Ideas," **National Review**, September 27, 1974, pp. 1095-99.

Cooper, Richard N., "Another Great Depression," **The New Republic**, March 29, 1975, pp. 17-21.

Crotty, James, and Raford Boddy, "Who Will Plan the Planned Economy?" **The Progressive**, February, 1975, pp. 15-19.

Curry, Leonard, "Bribes by the Millions: The Multi-national Corruption," **The Nation**, May 24, 1974, pp. 619-21.

Downie, Leonard Jr., "The Recreation Land Racket," **The Progressive**, May 1974, pp. 19-24.

Duscha, Julius, "Oil: The Data Shortage," **The Progressive**, February, 1974, pp. 23-25.

"Economics of the Defense Budget," **Business Week**, March 3, 1975, pp. 42-43.

Efron, Edith, "The Free Mind and the Free Market," **Vital Speeches**, June 15, 1974, pp. 522-27.

Entman, Robert and Clay Steinman, "The Sovereign State of Oil," **The Nation**, January 26, 1974, pp. 111-14.

Erwin, Robert, "Dead End: America on Wheels," **The Progressive**, December, 1974, pp. 15-20.

Flieger, Howard, "Profits — A Dirty Word," **U.S. News & World Report**, October 29, 1973, p. 104.

Froehlke, R.F., "Is an Armed Force Necessary Today?" **Vital Speeches**, March 1, 1974, p. 297.

Haslam, Gerald, "The Okies: Forty Years Later," **The Nation**, March 15, 1975, pp. 299-302.

Ignatius, David, "The Multinationals: Taming the Beast," **The New Republic**, September 14, 1974, pp. 15-19.

Jamison, C. Hayden, "Shareholders, Unite," **The Progressive**, July, 1974, pp. 24-27.

Kilpatrick, James J., "The Great Pledge," **Nation's Business**, October, 1974, pp. 11-12.

Kuortz, Herbert C., "The Multinational Corporation: An Economic Institution," **Vital Speeches**, June 15, 1974, pp. 535-40.

La Rocque, Gene R., "$100 Billion Military Budget," **Harper**, March, 1975, p. 8.

Lekachman, Robert, "The House is Burning: Notes on a Three Alarm Economy," **The Nation**, April 5, 1975, pp. 395-99.

Lens, Sidney, "Running Out of Everything," **The Progressive**, October, 1974, pp. 15-21.

Lens, Sidney, "The Moral Roots of the New Despair," **The Christian Century**, February 26, 1975, pp. 192-96.

Malley, D.D., "Lawrence Klein and His Forecasting Machine," **Fortune**, March, 1975, pp. 152-56 + .

Manne, Henry G., "Competition, Controls and Catastrophe," **Vital Speeches**, February 1, 1974, pp. 242-45.

McDonnell, Lynda, "Mobile Boxes of Ticky-Tacky," **The Progressive**, May, 1974, pp. 25-28.

"Military Regimes: Comparison of Military Expenditures," **National Review**, March 14, 1975, pp. 262-63.

Miller, Judith, "The Buying of America," **The Progresssive**, May, 1974, pp. 42-44.

Mirsky, Mark J., "Destroyers of the Dream," **The Progressive**, May, 1974, pp. 32-34.

Mylander, Maureen, "Fear of the Generals," **The Nation**, April 12, 1975, pp. 429-33.

"New Ear for Multinationals," **Business Week**, July 6, 1974, pp. 73-74.

Ognibene, Peter J., "Pentagon Prosperity," "The Defense Budget," **The New Republic**, February 22, 1975, pp. 10-11.

Rifkin, Jeremy, "George III, Inc.," **The Progressive**, July, 1974, p. 28.

Rogge, Benjamin A., "Will Capitalism Survive? A Diagnosis, Not a Prescription," **Vital Speeches**, July 1, 1974, pp. 564-68.

Russell, Bruce M. and Betty C. Hanson, "How Corporate Executives See America's Role in the World," **Fortune**, May, 1974, p. 165 + .

"Simon's Campaign to Curb Big Government," **Nation's Business**, February, 1975, pp. 18-21.

Smaby, Alpha, "The CAPUR Crusade," **The Progressive**, July, 1974, pp. 19-23.

Smith, J. Stanford, "Competition, Not Controls," **Vital Speeches**, February 1, 1974, pp. 247-48.

"Somewhere in the Promised Land," **Commonweal**, February 28, 1975, pp. 419-21.

Stern, Philip N., "Oil Profits: Where the Loot Goes," **The New Republic**, March 2, 1974, pp. 18-19.

"The Big Oil Slick," **The Nation**, February 16, 1974, p. 196.

"The Economics of the Defense Budget," **Business Week**, March 3, 1975, p. 42.

"The Oil Monopoly Myth," **Human Events**, February 2, 1974, p. 19.

Thompson, Mayo J., "Morality and Free-Enterprise," **Vital Speeches**, January 15, 1974, pp. 202-205.

Townsend, Lynn, "A Better Understanding of a Capitalist Society," **Vital Speeches**, June 15, 1974, pp. 540-42.

"Wastrel of the Western World," **The New Republic**, January 5 & 12, 1974, pp. 5-6.

Wells, Charles A., "Capitalism Betrayed," **Between the Lines**, January 15, 1975, p. 1.

"What to Do: Statement by Ten Experts," **Newsweek**, September 30, 1974, pp. 76-78.

Wilka, Mira, "Today Multinationals, Tomorrow the World," **Business Week**, February 10, 1975, p. 11.

SOCIAL JUSTICE

Brudnoy, David, "Fear and Loathing in Boston," **National Review**, October 25, 1974, pp. 1228-31.

Brudnoy, David and Ernest van den Haag, "Reflections on the Issue of Gay Rights," **National Review**, July 19, 1974, pp. 802-806.

Cohen, Carl, "The Defunis Case: Race & the Constitution," **The Nation**, February 8, 1975, pp. 135-45.

Coots, Max A., "On Abortion," **The Progressive**, November, 1974, pp. 20-21.

Curti, Josafat, "The Chicano and the Church," **The Christian Century**, March 12, 1975, pp. 253-57.

Evans, M. Stanton, "The ABC's of Busing," **Human Events**, October 13, 1973, p. 8.

"Exporting Anti-Semitism," **The New Republic**, March 15, 1975, pp. 5-7.

"Foes of Busing Step Up The Fight," **U.S. News & World Report**, March 11, 1974, p. 76.

Ford, Manrice de G., "The Schools: Detente in Boston," **The Nation**, May 3, 1975, pp. 518-21.

Gold, Victor, "Of Fallen Trees and Wounded Knees," **National Review**, April 27, 1973, p. 443.

Harris, Fred and La Donna, "Indians Coal and the Big Sky," **The Progressive**, November, 1974, pp. 22-26.

Hart, Jeffrey, "Whose Heart Was Really Buried at Wounded Knee?" **Human Events**, May 19, 1973, p. 17.

Kilpatrick, James J., "The Case Against the ERA," **Nation's Business**, January, 1975, pp. 9-10.

"Methodists Face the Homosexual Issue," **The Christian Century**, March 12, 1975, pp. 243-44.

"Pain in the Knee," **National Review**, May 11, 1973, p. 512.

Raskin, Marcus, "The System Impeached," **The Progressive**, September, 1974, pp. 15-18.

"Ratify the Equal Rights Amendment," **Nation's Business**, February, 1975, p. 15.

Reno, Philip, "The Navahos: High, Dry & Penniless," **The Nation**, March 29, 1975, pp. 359-72.

Riesel, Victor, "Chavez, Grapes and Lettuce," **Human Events**, June 1, 1974, p. 11.

Rogers, Cornish R., "Martin Luther King and the Bicentennial," **The Christian Century**, April 9, 1975, pp. 347-48.

"The Achievements of Elijah Muhammed," **The Christian Century**, March 26, 1975, pp. 301-02.

Van den Haag, Ernst, "Black Cop-Out," **National Review**, August 30, 1974, pp. 470-74.

Wall, James M., "Capital Punishment: A Moral Consensus?" **The Christian Century**, May 14, 1975, pp. 483-84.

Weidman, Judy, "Methodist Women Clergy Map Strategy," **The Christian Century**, February 26, 1975, pp. 188-89.

Well, Charles A., "The World of Wounded Knee," **Between the Lines**, May 1, 1973, p. 4.

JUSTICE AND FOREIGN POLICY

Baker, George L., "Good Climate for Agribusiness," **The Nation**, November 5, 1973, pp. 456-62.

"Big Job Ahead for U.S. — Holding on to Number One Spot," **U.S. News & World Report**, March 3, 1975, pp. 39-40.

Buckley, James L., "The Unconquerable Voice of the Human Conscience," **Vital Speeches**, February 15, 1974, pp. 262-65.

Butz, Earl L., "Who Will Speak for America?" **Vital Speeches**, September 15, 1974, pp. 710-12.

"Congress Dishonored by Brutal Viet Aid Cutoff," **Human Events**, March 29, 1075, p. 1 + .

Cox, David, "Reflections: On Amnesty," **The Progressive**, October, 1974, pp. 22-23.

Edwards, David V., "The Real Lessons of Vietnam," **The Nation**, May 10, 1975, p. 554.

Evans, M. Stanton, "The Ridiculous Crusade Against iTT," **Human Events**, May 5, 1973, p. 8.

Falk, Richard A., "Vietnam: The Final Deceptions," **The Nation**, May 17, 1975, p. 582.

"Ford Must Go to Mat On South Vietnam Aid,"
Human Events, February 8, 1975, p. 1 + .

"Ford's Cambodian Move a Breath of Fresh Air,"
Human Events, May 24, 1975, p. 1 + .

"4 Measures of World Economic Power," **U.S. News &
World Report**, March 3, 1975, p. 41.

"Fresh Look at How U.S. Power Stacks Up Against
Russia, China," **U.S. News & World Report**, March 3,
1975, pp. 55-56.

Goodpast, A.J., "Military Assistance Program: A
Successful Product of Political-Military Engineering,"
Vital Speeches, April 15, 1974, pp. 389-93.

Grant, Zalin B., "It's That Kind of War: Mylai Was Not
an Isolated Incident," **The New Republic**, December
20, 1969, pp. 9-11.

Harrigan, Anthony, "The Failure of Nationalization,"
Vital Speeches, August 15, 1974, pp. 657-60.

Kennedy, M. David, "War and the American Character," **The Nation**, May 3, 1975, pp. 522-26.

Knowl, Erwin, "The Mysterious Phoenix Project," **The
Progressive**, February, 1970, pp. 19-20.

Lanich, Frank, "The Missionary Who Knew Too
Much," **The Christian Century**, January 15, 1975, pp.
27-28.

Lens, Sidney, "Partners: Labor and the CIA," **The
Progressive**, February, 1975, pp. 35-39.

Lens, Sidney, "Vietnam: How It Really All Began,"
The Progressive, June, 1973, pp. 20-24.

Ligonier, John, "Will CIA Survive Anti-Intelligence
Mania?" **Human Events**, January 11, 1975, p. 1.

"Loyal Opposition: Views of Moynihan," **Time**, March
10, 1975, p. 10.

MacEoin, Gary, "How the CIA's 'Dirty Tricks' Threaten Mission Efforts," **The Christian Century**, March 5, 1975, pp. 217-23.

Maheu, Rene, "The Establishment of a New Economic Order," **UNESCO Courier**, November, 1974, pp. 20-24.

"Mideast Peace," **The New Republic**, March 8, 1975, pp. 3-8.

Miller, Judith, "Criminal Negligence: Congress, Chile, and the CIA," **The Progressive**, November, 1974, pp. 15-19.

"On the Disasters of the Indochina War," **The New Republic**, May 3, 1975. (Entire issue devoted to an analysis of Indochina War.)

Pirie, Madsen, "The Tiger Cages Revisited," **National Review**, September 27, 1974, p. 1103.

Rafferty, Max, "We Should Hear It for America," **Human Events**, November 17, 1073, p. 9.

Riesel, Victor, "Americans Need Not Be Ashamed of ITT vs.Marxism," **Human Events**, May 19, 1973, p. 19.

Sinclair, Gordon, "Let's Hear It for U.S.," **U.S. News & World Report**, November 19, 1973, p. 120.

Sisco, Joseph J., "American Foreign Policy Agenda: Toward the Year 2000," **Department of State Bulletin**, February 10, 1975, pp. 182-87.

"Sullivan, Flood Fear Panama Canal Giveaway," **Human Events**, March 1, 1975, p. 11.

Szulc, Tad, "U.S. and ITT in Chile," **The New Republic**, June 30, 1973, pp. 21-23.

"The Greatest Tragedy of All," **Time**, April 9, 1971, p. 13.

"The Terrible Realities: Letters from a G.I. in Vietnam," **The Progressive**, January, 1970, pp. 14-18.

Theodoracopulos, Taki, "The Anti-American Campaign," **National Review**, September 13, 1974, p. 1040.

meet
the editor

GARY E. McCUEN is a former high school social studies teacher. He received his A.B. in history from Ripon College, and has an M.S.T. degree in history from Wisconsin State University in Eau Claire, Wisconsin.